Norwood

GEM·OF·THE·HIGHLANDS·
·THE·BRIGHTEST·JEWEL·IN·

NORWOOD

Her Homes and Her People.

PLEASANT PLACES IN THE GEM OF THE HIGHLANDS.

A HISTORICAL SKETCH OF THE LIVELIEST MEMBER OF CINCINNATI'S SUBURBAN FAMILY

BY

REN MULFORD Jr., AND WERTER G. BETTY.

Embellished with Many Illustrations.

1894.

Copyrighted April 1891
By Mulford & Betty

NORWOOD.

TEN YEARS ago the Norwood of today be comparatively a part of the dreams of a few hopeful souls who believed that the future had much in store for a borough as abundantly blessed by nature. The pasture lands and orchards of the last decade have disappeared, and in their stead is a beautiful little city of homes linked to the Queen of the West by bands of iron and strands in which play the mystic forces of electricity. Norwood, among the youngest members of Cincinnati's sylvan family, has put on metropolitan airs. Her house is in order that she bids welcome to all of mankind who can appreciate what pluck and energy can do in the cause of progress.

There was a time, not many years ago, when Norwood was unknown—unnamed. The little handful of half a dozen homes on the Montgomery pike was called Sharpsburg. It never created much of a stir in the world. Farmers, on their way to and from the city, stopped at the old tavern, where there was cheer for both man and beast. Later on, the Marietta and Cincinnati railroad was built, and the primitive iron horse snorted and tugged up a heavy grade and stopped at the modest little Sharpsburg station that stood near where the Montgomery pike bridge is now located—a bridge that was built when the cut was made and travel rendered easier. Those whose memory long antedates the building of the railroad tell of the tavern on the hill—"Mother Goose's"—a famous resting place for the travelers along the old pike that was then the highway between Cincinnati, Chillicothe and Columbus.

When in 1869 the William Ferguson Farm, known as Norwood Heights, passed into the hands of the late S. H. Parvin, C. F. F. Lane and Belles, "Sharpsburg" was the adopted name of territory. That was not considered pretty enough for such a spot, and the suggestion of Mr. and Mrs. Parvin to call it Norwood (an abbreviation of Northwood) went into effect, and so it was that the suburb is christened now. This was the first of the subdivisions, but the hopes and plans of those early projectors were not carried out. The William R. Phipps home, now occupied by A. O. Russell, was the only building erected, and the trend of improvement shifted from hill top to valley, when L. C. Hopkins appeared upon the scene. The dry goods jobber soon further interests over to A. G. Hodapp and Louis G. Hoyer and to their careful handling of the property that had acquired is largely due the character of Norwood population.

From none of the hills that skirt the Avondale like gem, nowhere is there presented a panorama grander, grander than that which unfolds before the pilgrim who has scaled the heights that are crowned the historic Indian mound. Here, upon soil that a centuries ago sacred to the Red man, Norwood is raises up a monument to man's ingenuity and the progressive spirit of a suburb that has challenged the attention of all its neighbors. It is a spot which must have been fashioned when Dame Nature was in one of her merriest moods. Directly below one is the nestling villa surrounding of Pleasant Ridge. From the lake in the great west tower the beauty of the scene imposing. Village after village is one view beyond the ridge, one looks down upon Kennedy Heights, made prominent by Vonderlan, whose hospitable roof seems to cover the entire edge of the plateau upon which it has been built. The dim towers of Hartwell and Wyoming are visible, with Reading close enough to warrant the claim that they are triplets. Of the hamlets on the heights College Hill is prominent. Yet is the valley, to the left, seemingly nestling at the foothills of the range beyond

THE BLAKE HOMESTEAD, CAMERON AVENUE.

Millcreek, lie Hartwell, Cottages, Elmwood Place and Ivorydale. The square tower of the County Infirmary and the great dome of Longview Asylum loom up in the distance, lending an additional architectural charm to the scene, but those mighty walls echo the lamentations of disappointed lives and the cryings of others in whom the light of reason has been snuffed out. One sad thought to the fate of the unfortunates there and the eye sweeps onward. Bond Hill is a conspicuous figure in this magnificent picture. Far away the smoke-stacks of the tanneries that have given Ivorydale international repute are visible. Ludlow Grove and Clintonville both in sight and between the two St. Bernard lies, the clustered tombstones glistening in the sunlight in the cemeteries there, proving a grim reminder that Death lies in ambush everywhere. The twin spires that rise in the distance far in the distance give St. George's and Corryville a conspicuous place in the picturesque view. Then there is Mt. Auburn beyond. Sweeping away to the left is Walnut Hills, that great city of the hilltops, the Eden

tinted reservoirs beyond the Observatory, its water tanks elevated on stilts is conspicuous. Kentucky hills burst into view to the Southeast, but Bellevue is the only borough that can be seen in the old Commonwealth. Ft. Thomas, however, is within range of naked eye, and with the glass the stars and stripes of "Old Glory" can be seen flying in the breeze above a tower that towers at Uncle Sam's military station.

Norwood itself lies under this so almost metropolis. Plenty appears to be a confidante of pretty residences reaching almost to the gates of the city. The oft repeated cry that has nearly every thoroughfare as evidence in concert of the villagers' escape from the dulldom of bad walks. Hopkins avenue winds its way up the hillside, the artery that leads to Avondale. Avondale is a neighbor that is already touching elbows with the Bonded folks. The Montgomery road is a confidant of the scenery. Bloody Run, ugly only in a name, flows peacefully along the outskirts of town, keeping to itself the legend of the Indian massa-

Norwood is essentially a village of today. There are less than fifty of the inhabitants who can claim a residence of a quarter of a century. Edward Mills' grandfather was host at the old tavern, now the Sinker House, but modern improvements have obliterated nearly all traces of the honored landmark. Columbus Wilbraim, Thomas Drake, W. B. Fergusson, Moses F. Buxton, Emos Van Middlesworth, David Woodley, Justus Durrell and Rev. Jas. Lyon, famous as a farmer preacher, were among these pioneers. Some of their descendants have fallen in with the procession and aided in the development

of their old farm lands; but the "new blood" has proved the bone and sinew of the movement. Uncle Joe Langdon took up his residence here in 1850, and he tells of an incident in making a clearing which recalled Mad Anthony Wayne's campaign. In the heart of an Oak tree he found buried a bullet that had been hidden there than seven years.

In all of Cincinnati's suburban family there never was a more precocious youngster than Norwood. It early evidenced a disposition to leave the nursery in the possession of other sylvan sisters a bit older, but evincing quite so much pluck and energy. Before there were active steps taken toward incorporation the town was fairly well lighted. Back in those old days every division of territory has had at its improvement society. South Norwood was the pioneer in the movement, and East Norwood followed. Both West Norwood and old Norwood imbibed the spirit of progress, and it made

time to so much for Norwood it was evident that hopes for greater improvements lay in incorporation. The sentiment of the community was overwhelmingly in favor of such action, and on May 10, 1888, the efforts of A. C. Bedale and Casper H. Rowe, who had been named as agents for incorporation, were successful. Norwood celebrated her sixth birthday in 1894. Her record is one which must be a matter of personal pride to every soul within the corporate limits.

At the first municipal election—a special one, held August 11, 1888—190 votes were cast. At the last presidential election in 1892, four years later, that total had increased over five fold, and 1,026 citizens cast their ballots at the two precincts. Dr. John C. Weyer was the first mayor chosen; John C. Maxfer, treasurer; Edward G. Enlies, clerk, and Gerald Kehoe, marshal. The first board of councilmen was made up of Fred. H. Mehmert, Edward Mills, William Leser, J. P. Zim-

R. P. BELLSMITH, FOREST AND SMITH AVENUES.

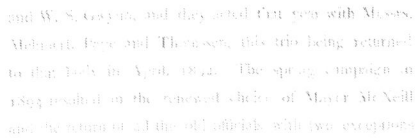

THE SERENADE OF PROSPERITY.

W. B. LINDSAY, CAMERON AVENUE.

NOT long ago a green brakeman was being "broken in" on "the big road," as every body calls the line over whose destinies Captain W. W. Peabody presides. The conductor, in the role of an instructor, was naming over the stations as the train rolled along. Norwood had scarcely been left behind when the raw knight of the lantern was coached to call out "East Norwood." Before he obeyed he gave a grunt of astonishment and remarked "Why don't they build a union depot out here?"

There are no less than six railroad stations within the limits of Norwood and right on the borders, scarce a stone's throw from the northern boundary line, are two more—Horewood and Norwood Heights—on the Chicago branch of the Pennsylvania, while away to the south the Cincinnati, Portsmouth and Virginia Road contributes two others to the list—Elsmere, which is within the corporate limits, and Idlewild, which is just without. The C., P. & V., which so long carried the title of the "Coot, Punts and Vest," now rejoices over the romantic name of "The Pocahontas Route."

Ivanhoe, Hopkins Avenue and Norwood Park are all on the Cincinnati, Lebanon and Northern, and East Norwood is the junction of the Highland Route and the Baltimore and Ohio Southwestern. On every day, but the Sabbath, nearly seventy passenger trains pass through Norwood and all save a few fast expresses stop. With such grand railroad accommodations it is easy to account for the healthy growth in the army of commuters. The shriek of the locomotive's whistle so often heard only swells the chorus in the serenade of prosperity. The old Marietta and Cincinnati ran her iron arms into Norwood when it was Sharpsburg and Ivineland. Not until years afterward was the Northern built and since President George Hafer assumed the reins of government and City Rockwell has been in charge of the passenger service, suburbanites on the Highland Route have been taken care of in good shape. The B. & O. S. W. has made a feature of suburban expresses, and O. P. McCarty, the G. P. A., has not over-

Not only has Norwood been extremely fortunate in the liberality of the steam railroads but there is another important artery of travel—the electric road on the Montgomery pike. From the day that the first car ran out over the Eden Park and Walnut Hills road to Norwood on the Fourth of July, not three years ago, the route has been a wonderfully successful one. Perhaps there was no one man in Norwood who did more toward having the road built than Fred Mehmert. Obstacles, such as the non-possession of a right of way, were removed by purchase outright of the pike. The Norwood Electric, with a five-cent through fare, proved a money maker from the start and it has been a large factor in the later-day growth of the borough. When the first cars were put on, the name "Norwood" could not be found on their sides even with the aid of a microscope, but a man at Fountain Square today can pick out a Norwood car without requiring the services of an interpreter. There are prophets who aver that before many years elapse the electric will circle on over the bridge and down Harris Avenue through East Norwood to the picturesque Duck Creek road and thence find an outlet into Norwood Park and return to Montgomery Boulevard through South Norwood. That, however, is only a promissory note for Norwood has a singular faculty of taking up all such booty notes and paying them off.

THE MAYOR AND HIS CABINET.

THE OFFICIAL FAMILY.

NORWOOD has been superlatively fortunate in the choice of her officers, and from the time of the selection of the first members of the village cabinet to the present hour. Dame Scandal has not had a chance to whisper a word of suspicion. Mayor Aaron McNeill, who is serving his second term, is a member of the law firm of Archer & McNeill. He is a Muskingum County product and has long been prominent in the councils of Ohio. Grand Lodge of the I. O. O. F. He is one of Norwood's heavy weights, physically and intellectually. In Cincinnati he ranks with the notably successful practitioners of the bar, and he has lent dignity, ability and an intense loyalty to everything Norwood to his administration.

FREDERICK H. MEHMERT, MONTGOMERY BOULEVARD

John C. Masker is the only treasurer Norwood has ever had, and his term is likely to last as long as he is willing to hold the village purse strings. Mr. Masker is a retired manufacturer, and for nearly a quarter of a century he was a member of the Cincinnati soap and candle house of B. H. Lamping & Co. He has proved a faithful officer in this, the first public position to which his fellow townsmen called him.

That is a characteristic trait of Norwood officials. The great majority of them began their public careers in the great cause of Norwood's prosperity, and take pride of Norwood's in the length, depth, breadth and height of their political ambition. W. E. Wichgar, who has served as clerk since 1891, is the right man in the right place. He writes a hand as clear as copper plate, and is with the American Book Company. W. L. Brady, the solicitor, has proved to be an adept in diplomacy in handling the legal affairs of the village. Before he came to Norwood he served as Secretary of the Board of Elections of Hamilton County. Some years ago he edited the Wellston Argus and the Ohio Mining Journal. His father was killed fighting for the flag of the Union, and when he was chosen Colonel of the Sons of Veterans of the State of Ohio, he repeated then title. He was also Province President of the Phi Delta Theta. Colonel Brady's grandfather, H. S. Brady, is the oldest man in Congress, and Norwood's side for an man who is a credit to his ancestry.

There is but one member of the Board of Council who has served the village faithfully and continuously ever since its birth. Councilman Frederick H. Mehmert. He is treasurer of the L. L. Dessauer Company in the clothing business in Cincinnati. He resides in the old L. C. Hoskins home on Montgomery Avenue, and "Old Norwood" has kept him in his seat. Reference to his missionary efforts on behalf of the electric road is made in another chapter. A. H. Pope, East Norwood's representative, ranks next in time of service. He is now secretary of the Chamber of Commerce in Cincinnati, has been on the railroad business for fifteen years, and is the agent of the C. & O. During the life of the Davenport Club house, a leading spirit, and at that time he ranked as one of the best of Cincinnati's amateur disciples of Thespis. West Norwood loses most her favorite son when John Rolan was sent to council, and since H. Colyer on that body

West Norwood has kept pace with every other section of the village in the character and scope of the improvements made. In business, he is with Knight & Co., the Cincinnati printers and publishers, and is serving his fourth year as a "city father." John J. Hess was called by the people on the Heights, and he did so well that they sent him back for a second term. He is a carriage builder and in business for himself in Cincinnati. Although born in Germany, only two years of his life was spent there. The Ivanhoe and Elsmere district has a worker in Albert Berger. "Good roads" is his hobby, and as a trustee of Millcreek Township, he rode it before he broadened his field of public endeavor. Mr. Berger is superintendent of the tank wagon system of the Standard Oil Company, and his acquaintance in Cincinnati is very large. He was in the oil business himself for ten years before joining forces with the Standard. Jacob M. Thomssen, who is with the Methodist Book Concern, was the only member of the old council who retired in the spring of 1894. He has been deservedly invested with the title of "the father of the water works movement," and there was no man in the body more active in the early advocacy of action along that line than he. After four years of service in the board, he decided to retire and Edward B. Anthony was elected to succeed him as South Norwood's representative. Although Norwood has never been divided into wards, it is the custom to give each one of the six divisions of territory membership in council. That is an unwritten law that has never been violated. Mr. Anthony is one of the best known of the old newspaper guard in Cincinnati. He has been on the Enquirer and Times-Star staffs, and now holds a position of trust under County Treasurer Leo Schott.

Colonel James M. Harper, the village engineer, was called to that post by council. He is well qualified for the duties of the important trust. For eight years he had served Hamilton County as chief engineer and he has been with various railroads centering in Cincinnati in the capacity of a civil engineer. The Ohio State Society of Surveyors and Civil Engineers, at its last session, complimented Colonel Harper by an election to the presidency of that important body. Pleasant Ridge, noting the skill with which Norwood's engineering was conducted, has installed Colonel Harper in the same position there. Too young to enlist he was an assistant under his father, Surgeon Harper, who was attached to Gen. Sherman's staff. In Norwood, John A. Murray, Andrew Birkhamm and Edward Hoel hold the rank of assistant engineers.

Marshal Benjamin Zeis has been titled "Norwood's Chief Deputy," for he combines the duties of a member of the "finest" with those of the position to which he was elected. He is a faithful official, and lives in his cozy home on Lawrence avenue.

A PEEP AT TIONESTA.

Nestling on the banks of Duck Creek is Tionesta — Norwood's stock farm. The farm is owned by A. C. Strobel and in charge of Charles Hazenfield. It is used under pick for training purposes. The trotting star of the stud is the Wilkes Simmons' stallion, Colonel Wood, who has the blood of Hambletonian and Mambrino Chief in his veins. Colonel Ren, a French coach horse, with a good pedigree, and the Major, a Shetland pony, are also noted

EDWARD B. ANTHONY.

THE PLATTING COMMISSION'S TASK.

DURING the summer of 1887 the Platting Commission was established. The idea was fathered in part by Philip Miesenger, who had had experience on a similar board in Cincinnati, and foresaw the urgent necessity of a similar work at Norwood. Drs. N. L. Scott, Prof. J. U. Lloyd, Dr. John C. Meyer, J. P. Marker and the late William Wieghorst were in the commission when organized August 15th. On account of other business engagements J. P. Lloyd tendered his resignation March 1st, and Dr. N. L. Scott March 16th, 1891, the resignations being accepted by council. The remaining members were dissatisfied with this course, and wishing to lose their members' services, and in consequence Mr. Lloyd reconsidered, but owing to increased duties, Dr. Scott found it impossible to serve. Mr. Lloyd was reappointed March 23rd, 1891, Mr. Samuel L. Harris being appointed at the same time to the vacancy occasioned by the retirement of Dr. Scott. The board at once organized by electing J. U. Lloyd chairman and Mr. W. H. Perry secretary, the former secretary, Mr. W. L. Wieghorst, having been elected village clerk. Mr. Wieghorst died September 20th, 1891, and on the November 21st, 1891, appointed Mr. E. L. Niermann to the vacancy, since which time no changes have been made. Of the great work done by the commission, Chairman Lloyd says:

"The duties of the Platting Commission have been arduous and often unpleasant. They found the territory embraced in the newly incorporated village to be composed of farm lands, additions, subdivisions and dedications in no respect conformable to each other or to the public at large. Farm property in many cases had been subdivided to meet the necessity of the owners individually, irrespective of the welfare of any others. Streets had been faintly dotted off on paper by some men, often to assist their own ends, and very frequently no pains were taken to make them conform with the welfare of the community. In some cases irregular shaped pieces of ground were purposely left as a matter of speculation, while in others the streets laid out by one party had been artfully blocked by another. These monuments to man's cupidity, irreparable in many cases, remain yet in many places an object lesson staring in the face of a growing people.

"Norwood, with her crazy-quilt topography, speaks volumes unanswerable in favor of a county platting commission with sweeping power that shall protect the generations that are to follow against the selfishness of those who have no higher duty to the land they live in than to make the most money out of their evanescent heirloom or speculative possession. The Platting Commission of Norwood has attempted with only moderate success to establish order out of this chaotic condition. The various sections have been united in the best manner possible under the circumstances, but still unsatisfactorily. A few streets have been widened, others straightened, a few vacated and many new streets platted. Council heartily entered into the work and numbers of condemnations of property for street purposes to benefit the community have followed, owners having reaped their harvest and relieved themselves of the obligation. The village has also suffered from this selfishness of speculators and inheritors of farm lands, and the tax payers of Norwood are collectively paying for property that should have been donated for street purposes."

"Well, Tom, how are you getting along at school?" asked Prof. J. U. Lloyd one evening of his young hopeful. The face of the youthful botanist clouded up and he grumbled: "I'd do pretty well if it wasn't for music. They ask a fellow such foolish questions."

"What are they?" inquired his father.

"Why, to-day they wanted to know how many stamps there were in a bushel!" was the astonishing information given. It took time to solve the mystery. The actual query which had caused the mischief was: "How many bars are there in a measure?"

THE BOARD OF IMPROVEMENTS.

WHEN this body cast its official vote over Norwood on the 14th of April, 1892, the date of its first meeting, very few presentable streets were sighted. Henry C. Meader and George E. Hipple were the members who acted with the mayor, but Mr. Hipple resigned and William Windhorst was chosen to fill the vacancy. The miles of improved streets and the legislation for the many more that are to follow is the overwhelming evidence that may be offered to prove the grand works this little board endorsed. Both gentlemen are as well and favorably known in Cincinnati as they are by their neighbors, Mr. Meader is the Fourth street ticket broker, and Mr. Windhorst, the dry goods merchant, a member of the Main street firm of Holmstedt & Windhorst.

Charles A. Ewing§ succeeded Mr. Holbrook as village engineer in May, 1891, and he held that position until June, 1892, when it was deemed advisable to secure a resident engineer, and James M. Harper was installed, and is still serving in that capacity. During Mr. Ewing's term the character of street improvements were changed from primitive form to those more befitting a municipality, and by the end of the season, $135,000 worth of improvements had been made under his supervision. Some idea of the wonderful strides Norwood has made in the cause of good streets and good sidewalks may be gained from figures which indicated the completed improvements up to March 15, 1894. Engineer Harper reported that at that time 1 5/8 miles of streets had been macadamized at a cost of $335,100.16, the average per foot being $2.83.26. Park and Floral avenues are the only asphalt streets in the village, and they  are 3400 feet long, $7.57 foot. Brick streets are not common in only part of a mile has been improved in this manner, at a cost of $6,283.36, or an average of $3.60.1.33 foot. Of curbstone walks there are 1 5/8 miles laid at a cost of $16,358.30. The average expense to property owners was $9.30.3 or a fraction less than half a dollar a foot.

At the time the report was made the improvements of Forest, Harris, Elm and Hudson avenues were under way. With the completion of the former thoroughfare once the solution of a problem that proved a perplexing one for several years. Forest avenue is now the connecting link between South and East Norwood. The means this afforded was evident, as territory have been filled up, and as of the most important of all the street public works in the life of the young village successfully completed to block, energy and perseverance. At the same time the water works jubilee takes place the fitting for East Norwood is about her younger sister for a fresh. All is ready for the wedding.

ORGANIZED LABOR.

Organized Labor has strong footholds in the village. One of the organizations of the kind in the Brotherhood of Union No. 735, of the Carpenters and Joiners of America. Here members only number 15. In good standing, and their officers are President C. L. Metcalfe, Vice-President J. P. Mean, Recording Secretary F. Peter, Financial Secretary A. J. Be

THE WATER WORKS PLANT.

AFTER months of agitation the people of Norwood were called upon on November 8, 1892, to vote upon the question of building a water works, and those in favor of the enterprise carried the day by the decisive figures of 491/467 and 158 against. The failure of tellers to arrive at the Ivanhoe precinct was responsible for the loss of at least one hundred votes. The issue of $40,000 worth of bonds was endorsed, but the work was of such a character that another appropriation of the same amount was asked for and granted by the people. Mayor McNeill appointed as water works trustees Dr. Alfred Springer, George Puchta and Henry Rikhoff, and under their direction has the enterprise been carried out. The nominees

DR. ALFRED SPRINGER, MONTGOMERY AND MOUND AVENUES.

of the mayor were confirmed by council and afterward elected unanimously by the suffrages of their fellow towns-

men. Mr. Rikhoff's term expiring, he was re-elected to the long term at the April election in 1894. At a time when panic threatened the land Norwood went boldly ahead, and during the darkest days of 1893, hundreds of men were at work on the water works contracts at the building, laying the mains, and at the foundry, where the steel plates for the tower were welded into shape. A test well was sunk to bed rock, fifty feet below the low water mark of the Ohio river at Cincinnati, distant on an air line three miles. The result proving satisfactory, the trustees felt justified in acquiring the property on Harris avenue, at the junction of the B. & O. S. W. and C. L. & N. railroads, and erecting the plant on that site. Six wells were drilled there. The first one, experimental, is six inches in diameter; the other five

The force [...] from the
[...] to the reservoir is
[...] of the distributing
mains through a [...] to
maintain the engine pressure, though cut 8 in 9, as is
at the reservoir. By the
closing and opening of the
proper valves the water can
be supplied in three ways.
First, by the direct pressure
from the pumps, the [...] of
connection being elsewhere; second, by the pressure above,
the direct motion of, closed
either at the foot of the hill
or at the reservoir; third, by
the reservoir and pumps
together, all valves being
opened. The distributing system has been arranged on
the grid-iron plan, water flowing to all mains from two directions, which insures a good
supply to the fire hydrants
and avoids cutting off the
supply for more than an

RESIDENCE ON NORWOOD AVENUE

[...] at a time for repairs. The boilers and pumping plant were manufactured and put in by the Laidlaw-Dunn-Gordon Co., of Cincinnati. The style of pumping engine is what is known as the compound condensing duplex pumping engine, and at a speed of 20 revolutions per minute, the aggregate capacity is 1,680,000 gallons in 24 hours. The high pressure cylinders are 11 inches in diameter, the low pressure cylinders, 18½ inches in diameter; the water cylinders, 10½ inches in diameter, and all of them 12 inch stroke. It is fitted with 10 inch suction and 8 inch discharge openings, and is rated as a high grade pumping engine. The steam cylinders are lagged with asbestos and Russia iron with brass bands to prevent condensation of steam. It is fitted with an automatic pressure regulating governor to control the speed of the pump in accordance with the pressure on the mains, and which stops the pump absolutely should all the valves on the water main be closed. This prevents undue pressure and breakage. The water end is fitted with an automatic pressure relief valve also to prevent undue pressure. The pumping engine has all the necessary revolution counters, combination pressure gauges, showing feet of water column and pounds of pressure on the pumping engine, and is fitted throughout in a first class manner. Connected with this, to give greater economy, is the Hill surface condenser with du-

plex air pump, into which the exhaust of the engine passes, and through brass tubes in which the discharge water from the main passes and condenses all the steam used from the pumping engine, the air or vacuum pump being used to take this condensation, pump it into the heaters and also to create a vacuum in the steam cylinders of the pumping engine.

There are also four vertical pumping engines on the four deep wells, the sizes of the engines being 10 inch steam cylinders with 36 inch stroke, having top brass bushing plungers 4½ inch diameter. These cylinders operate the working pump cylinders, which are placed down in the well, about 225 feet below the engine room floor. These deep-well pumping engines draw the water from the deep wells and pump it into a steel cistern

J. A. KNAPP, OAK STREET

20¼ feet in diameter and 13¼ feet high, of 36,294 gallon capacity, resting upon the concrete floor of the engine house. From this the large pumping engine takes its supply and forces the water from the mains to the town and reservoir, 2050 feet distant through 12 inch pipe. The steam pump feeding the boilers is of the well known duplex type. It is used for taking the hot water from the heater and forcing it into the boiler. There is also another vertical air pump which is used for priming the air vessels of the large pumping engine with air. There are two boilers which are rated at about 125 horse power each. They are 66 inches in diameter by 18 feet long, and are known as horizontal stationary return tubular boilers. Each boiler has 64 lap welded tubes, 4 inch diameter. The boilers have been thoroughly inspected by the insurance companies, and are insured for $500 each for one year. They are trimmed with all the latest appliances, such as gauges, gage cocks, water columns, and each has an injector that safely feeds each boiler is guaranteed to be of sufficient capacity to supply the two deep well pumps and one compound engine working together, with a consumption of coal of each guaranteed not to exceed 250 pounds per hour. The heater also referred to of the latest design, and is used for the double purpose of heating the water and purifying it before it is pumped into the boiler. All the

Everything has been done to insure a first-class plant. The setting of the boilers is of the latest design, to insure economy and prevent smoke.

On the brow of East Norwood Heights rests the water tower, 100 feet in height. A stairway from Forest avenue makes it easily accessible from East Norwood, and the carriage drive out Montgomery and Mound avenues is a pleasant one. The great steel structure was put up by the Stacey Manufacturing Co. The foundation or substructure upon which the water tower was built, rests upon the natural heavy yellow clay, and at a depth of eleven and one-half feet beneath the natural surface, rock was found in alternating strata of from three to six

inches in thickness. The bottom of the water tower rests upon concrete foundation ten feet thick, composed of four parts screened broken stone, two parts of sand and one part of cement used promptly after mixing, and put down in four or six layers and thoroughly rammed with wooden rammers. The surface of each layer was well sprinkled with water before the next one was laid. The coping upon which the outer perimeter of the tank rests consists of Bedford (Indiana) stone, each block being two feet wide, two feet thick, and four feet long, laid and bedded in cement. The upper surface of the coping was accurately dressed to fit the cylindrical slope of the water tower. The brick work in the valve chambers was laid in cement mortar. No broken brick were used, only where it was necessary to effect a closure. The steel plates used in the construction of the tower were made by the Corbin Steel Company of Pittsburg, Pa., and are of 6,000 pounds tensile strength, tough, ductible, uniform in quality, and incapable of tempering. The material was subjected to the most rigid and exacting inspection and tests, and in all instances conformed to the very strict requirements of the specifications. The trace of phosphorus discovered in the metal did not exceed $\frac{1}{100}$ of one per cent. The elongation of the eight inch test pieces was in no instance less than twenty-five per cent. Pieces were bent cold and doubled flat on themselves without exhibiting a sign of fracture on the convex side. Tests were made by bringing the steel to a uniform bright cherry red heat, then cooled in water, and bending around a circle of a diameter equal to 1½ times the thickness of test pieces without showing fracture. The bottom plates

THE WATER TOWER.

joints and connected together with 5/8 inch rivets and joined to the first or lower course of side plates with 6 x 6 x 3/8 inch angles. This bottom course rests upon a bed two inches thick of a dry mixture of two parts of sand and one of Portland cement, evenly spread over the concrete foundation. The bottom of the water tower is firmly secured to the stone coping by 32 anchor bolts 1 inch thick by 12 inches long, passing into the coping. The first or lowest course of side plates is 5/8 inch thick; second course is 1/2 inch; third course, 7/16 inch; fourth course, 3/8 inch. These four courses are butt jointed and secured by butt plates 15 1/2 inches wide and of the same thickness as the plates in the corresponding course, and all are triple riveted with rivets one inch in diameter. The fifth course is 5/16 inch thick; sixth course, 1/4 inch; seventh course, 3/16 inch; eighth course, 3/16 inch. The ninth, tenth, eleventh and twelfth courses are 3/16 inch thick. All of the plates are butt jointed and secured by butt plates, double riveted. Around the upper edge of the top course are placed two rings of 3 x 3 x 3/8 inch angles, one on the inside and one outside of the plates, all securely riveted together, thus forming with the angle

JOHN C. MASKER, MILLS AVENUE

and channel at the roof cornice over the gallery a trussed ring calculated to resist the wind pressure on the roof and on the side of the tower for a depth of three feet.

The water tower is surmounted with a roof, formed with channel and trussed rafters that are rigidly connected with two tiers of horizontal struts, and a forged ring at the top and bolted to the flange angles at sides of the tower. This frame is covered with steel plates 1/8 inch thick—the whole forming a true cone. A substantial ornamental stairway, three feet wide, encircling the tower, is attached to wrought iron brackets, securely bolted to the side, leading to a gallery or promenade around the tower, placed eight feet below a cylindrical top. The tower is built with a factor of safety of four for the hydrostatic pressure, and a factor of three for a wind pressure of 200 pounds per square foot. Measurements accurately made after the tower was completed showed it to be exactly forty feet inside diameter at both bottom and top. A plumb suspended from the center of the roof system to bottom of tower varied 1/2 of an inch from the exact

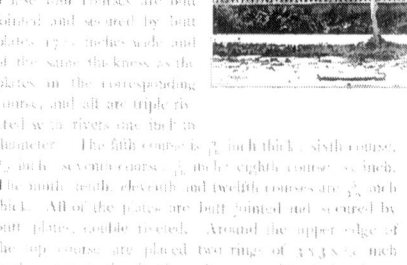

center. The body of the structure is painted a stone, the roof a moss, and the stairway a slate color. Its dimensions and color render it a very conspicuous object for miles in every direction. The bottom or floor line of the tower is 378 4/12 feet above low water in the Ohio river, and is 186 4/12 feet above the bottom of the small tank in the pumping house, giving a water pressure of 81 pounds per square inch on the floor level of the engine house, and a pressure of 103 pounds per square inch from the overflow line, 56 feet and 8 inches above the bottom. The capacity of the tower to the overflow line is 512,666 gallons, which affords four days' supply for a population of 4,000 at the rate of 25 gallons per head, or a supply for eight one and one-quarter inch fire nozzles working simultaneously for five hours.

The builders of the pumping station were W. H.

WILLIAM WINDHORST, WILLIAMS AVENUE

Stewart's Sons. Hebert and Lapayre were the contractors who laid all the mains, using the output of the Addyston Pipe Works. The Bourbon Brass and Copper Works furnished all the fire plugs and brass valves.

It was Dr. Springer who was the earliest advocate of the steel tower. That was a pet project of his. Others made plans for the lower pressure system, but the doctor's arguments prevailed, and he and his successor, indeed when he was named for the long term and reelected chairman of the water works, found by his associates in that body. Around the tower a driveway has been made. The park upon which the tower is built, with the Indian mound, is destined to be one of the most popular little parks in the village—the more for it sightseers who are searching for the point of vantage from which is afforded the grandest views in the county. The mound of piles or redskins, long since called by the Great Father to the Happy Hunting Grounds, is held in trust for generations to come. The level knoll is crested with forest trees, and the guardians, under the terms of the dedication, are pledged to make but excavations save for the planting of trees and shrubbery. Over

THE MONTGOMERY BOULEVARD.

THERE is scarcely a man within the confines of the borough who has not constituted himself a member of the "Welfare Committee." Everybody is for Norwood, but in November, '93, council, by resolution, invested eleven citizens with that official title. F. W. Jewell was chosen chairman by his associates, A. H. Pape, H. C. Meader, J. M. Thomssen, Albert Berger, W. E. Wichgar, John W. Hall, C. J. Kemper, J. C. Lloyd and Charles E. Prior. Mayor McNeill was also made a member ex officio, and W. S. Gwynn was pressed into harness as secretary. No specific duties have been outlined for the Welfare Committee, but any project that augurs well for Norwood's good will fare well at its hands. There was much rejoicing when the Seventieth General Assembly passed the original bill for the Montgomery Boulevard, under the provisions of which J. C. Lloyd and Albert McCullough were appointed as trustees to supervise the improvement. Legal obstacles were thrown in the way, and when the Supreme Court declared the bill unconstitutional the masses in the cause of a good road simply inaugurated another crusade. The Welfare Committee nursed the new bill, which was fathered by

ALBERT McCULLOUGH.

Senator Rump, and it passed both houses—not, however, before the Hamilton County delegation had been bumped, thumped and dumped over the road destined to be a boulevard eighty feet wide, which was a compromise between the advocates of a 100-foot and a 70-foot road from Walnut Hills to the B. & O. S. W. bridge. The improvement is to be either brick or asphalt, as the County Commissioners select, and from that point to Main avenue the roadway will be macadam. A Committee on "Push" was appointed during the week the bill became a law, and to Henry Feldcamp, W. W. Peasell, Col. W. E. Bundy, Dr. W. D. Hopkins, Harris O. Geneva, Fred Mehmert, Benjamin Franklin Smith and Edward Mills was entrusted the work preliminary to the building of the finest thoroughfare in the State of Ohio.

ONLY A POSTAL NOTE.

When Norwood was raised to the estate of the new born village, Uncle Sam got out the pen and scratched Sharpsburg off his list of post offices in Ohio. Congressman Bellamy Storer interested himself in behalf of a free postal delivery for Ivorydale-Elmwood, this part of the First District, and he succeeded. Three carriers, one mounted and two afoot, made one delivery and two collections every day. There are two stations, with other conveniences of the borough. J. L. Vincent declares meritorious at Norwood Station and Lee Cossell looks after the interest of the Ivorydale station. Money orders are the business of either office, and both are special delivery stations.

THE SEWERAGE DISTRICTS.

THE natural drainage of Norwood was fairly good, but the question of sewerage—such an important adjunct to health—was entrusted to a commission in June, 1891. The problem before them was no easy one, but the village has been divided into four districts, the first of which, in East Norwood, was completed in the fall of 1893, at a cost of a little over $26,000, and of that assessment more than $5,000 was paid in cash. Elsmere comprises one of the other districts, South Norwood a third, and Central and West Norwood the fourth. A. H. Singer is the only member of the original commission who is not now on the board. He was succeeded, after his short term, by Peter Betinger, who is chairman. The others are Edward Mills, N. Ashley Lloyd, J. M. Harper and E. Bolles, who fills the post of secretary. The commission has labored earnestly and most faithfully, and their work of vast interest to the whole community, has been well done. The system of sewerage is one that has been tried and no doubt wanting. The first or separating system which was adopted is successful operation in several eastern cities. Automatic flushing basins are located at the mouth of each lateral sewer, and under these conditions it will be impossible to choke up subterranean drainage. The plans of Chas. A. Ensign serve to our adopted and under his administration, the great work now in progress will be fulfilled.

N. ASHLEY LLOYD, HARRIS AVENUE

THE FOES OF DISEASE.

... call for a convention of the health officers of the State. "Columbus!" observed his young son, Leon, and, with an emphasis which closed further study and wonder. "How can you go to Columbus? He's been dead a thousand years!"

The health of Norwood is a matter of concern to all its inhabitants. Since the establishment of the Board of Health with its far-reaching regulations, which are enforced without fear or favor, infectious diseases have not run riot through the village. Dr. Tidball has filled the post of health officer ever since the creation of the board. His report for the year of 1893 showed fifty-eight deaths, a rate less than twelve in one thousand. W. L. Zeller and C. E. Page are the only ex-members of the board, which now consists of Mayor McNeal, ex-officio, W. M. Langdon, chairman; S. S. Kingery, J. A. Knapp, W. A. Stewart, A. A. Brown and Dr. E. C. Wintermute.

The board, in all its good works, has

THE VILLAGE OF CHURCHES.

LONG before Norwood was dignified with a place on the map the good people of the country roundabout were wont to meet on the Sabbath at the old school house, and there, regardless of creed, worshiped the Giver of all things. When Henry Ward Beecher was a young student at Lane Seminary, he used to walk out and join in these services of praise. With the building of the public hall that edifice afforded opportunities for the formation of embryonic congregations. To-day, Norwood is aptly called "The Village of Churches." Within its boundaries nine sanctuaries are to be found and the spires of Norwood's spiritual temples rear their tapered heads toward heaven, monuments to a higher civilization and evidences of the abounding faith in the Great Ruler of the Universe.

GEORGE F. DAVIS JR., WILLIAMS AVENUE.

Harris Avenue M. E. Church.

There were just thirteen in the little class organized on the 31st of August, 1884, by the Rev. Dr. D. J. Starr, presiding elder of the East Cincinnati district. Rev. G. L. Luffer, of Pleasant Ridge, took pastoral charge, and the following January the first steps toward a church home was taken, when Mrs. E. Woodley, John Woodley and his wife, Mary M. Woodley, John Arnold and Mrs. A. V. Arnold deeded the lot upon which the sanctuary now stands. Ground was broken in August, and on May 2, 1886, the church was dedicated. Rev. E. E. Lane was then pastor, and since that time the spiritual welfare of the congregation has been directed by the Revs. George E. Johnson, R. E. Officer, Thomas J. Harris, Wesley H. Benham, J. A. Fahnor and George V. Morris. The latter is now in charge. There are eight organizations within

EDWARD C. RUNGE, NORWOOD AVENUE AND MARION STREET.

the church, the Sunday School, Missionary Society, Ladies' Aid Society, Taylor Chapter of the Epworth League, Junior League, Woman's Home and Foreign Missionary Societies, and the Y. M. M. L. From the original number the membership has increased almost tenfold. The present officers are: Trustees—S. B. Markland, W. E. Zoller, A. F. Hollis, A. P. Hagemeyer, W. G. Williams, F. W. Richter, Wm. Borcherding, Jas. Neeb and B. Frank Smith. Stewards—S. B. Markland, W. E. Zoller, A. F. Hollis, A. P. Hagemeyer, W. G. Williams, J. E. Hattersley, D. G. Zoller, Henry Borcherding, George Shinard and C. M. Flowers. D. G. Zoller, Recording Steward and Treasurer.

St. Elizabeth Congregation, Catholic.

This congregation, one of the youngest in the diocese of Cincinnati, has shown a most remarkable growth. Its beginning may be dated to 1884, when, on the 31st of August, a number of Catholics met at the house of J. S. Bokenkotter, and there founded St. Joseph's Catholic Men's Society of Norwood. Messrs. Mills and Klin do-

nated some lots on Carter and Mills Avenue to the Society for church purposes. On October 6, 1884, the Society was incorporated. By the collection of dues, subscriptions, raffles, and other means, a sufficient sum was realized for the building of the first church, which contained under the same roof, school rooms and parsonage. This building was dedicated on October 5, 1886, by the Very Rev. Vicar General J. C. Albrinck, Ph. D., who, on pain will others thereafter, celebrated mass on Sundays only. The congregation being small in number, and therefore unable to support a pastor regularly. The first resident pastor was the Rev. Jos. Steppelmann, who took charge on the 23d of October 1887. School was first opened in December of that year. In January following, Father Steppelmann became seriously ill and remaining so for some months, Rev. J. B. Kayser succeeded him as pastor. Under his care, the congregation experienced great growth. In the fall of 1888 a large, roomy parsonage was erected. In 1891 the old church was enlarged, so as to accommodate the increased membership. The new addition was blessed by the Most Rev. Archbishop W. H. Elder, on the 25th of October. In the

owing to ill-health [...]
[...]. As his successor
the Rev. Jos.
M. [...] was appointed.

The congregation now
numbers [...] families.
The splendid schools are in
charge of eight Sisters of
Charity.

Societies attached to the
church include St. Joseph
Men's, St. Leo Men's, St.
Raphael Young Men's, St.
Elizabeth Married Ladies'
Young Men and Boys So-
dality, Young Ladies and
Girls sodality, St. Cecilia
Young Ladies' Domestic Art
[...] Altar Society, Young
Men's Literary Association,
and Third Order of St.
Francis.

The excellent choir is
directed by J. Meyer. The
present trustees of the congregation are Messrs. H. H.
Baer, P. J. Schueler, H.
[...], John Robert, F. [...], Theo. Lohman and
Joseph Espel.

The Ivanhoe Methodists.

EARLY in 1884, a little mission Sunday school was started
by Rev. J. W. Kirkell at the Ivanhoe depot, and
from that origin has grown the Ivanhoe M. E. Church.

In June of the following year the modest little sanctuary
on Ivanhoe avenue, was dedicated, and since that time
Revs. G. W. Hammell and A. E. Austin have been in
charge. The Rev. D. C. Washburn is the present pastor.
Within the church are the Woman's Home Missionary So-
ciety, the Ladies' Circle, the Willing Workers and the
Epworth League. The Trustees are W. C. Baker, W. H.
Buckton, A. J. Chapple,
David Davis, John G. Evans,
C. E. Lindsey, E. W. Jewell,
C. E. Prior and Dr. John
Weyer. The Stewards are
A. J. Chapple, W. R. Locke,
A. C. Roberts, G. W. Hurd
and Dr. Weyer. The con-
gregation is a growing one
and they are proud of a
bright interior.

The Presbyterian Congre-
gation.

THE May Queen witnessed
the birth of the Presby-
terian Church in 1887, for
before the organization was
effected there were meetings
addressed by Rev. J. H. Walter, who came over from
the Ridge. While pursuing
his studies at [...] seminary

The Baptist Harmon

T

The Berean Baptists.

The Berean Baptist Church was organized in Cincinnati, June 15, 1873, with a membership of thirteen, John E. Morris being called to the pastorate. The people met at first in Hopkins Hall, corner Fourth and Elm streets, and subsequently in other places in the city. In October, 1877, Mr. Morris resigned and went to Chicago, but in 1880, he was recalled, and remained with them until the fall of 1893, when he again responded to a Chicago call. Since that time services have been conducted by the members. In the autumn of 1890, the church held its meetings in Mission Hall, Norwood, when in May, 1891, Joseph G. Langdon generously donated the lot on Smith avenue on which stands their edifice. The church now,

having a pleasant home, is taking on new life; the membership and congregation steadily increasing. They have a flourishing Sunday school of which Philip Straus is superintendent. The building cost $6,500. The trustees are W. M. Langdon, Philip Straus, Louis Schneider, Alvin Langdon and Francis Wenz. Mr. Wenz being also the builder.

Mission of the Good Shepherd.

The Mission of The Good Shepherd of the Episcopal Church was organized June 23, 1891, at the residence of Geo. H. Bonte, with a membership of fifteen, and an executive committee composed of Geo. H. Bonte, J. S. Tompkins, Geo. Fuller, H. L. Harrington and J. R. Lindsey. Very soon thereafter an eligible lot, corner of Ashland and Monroe avenues, was secured for $1,195, and during the following year a church building was erected thereon at a cost of $4,055. The first service was held in the new building early in July, 1892. Services had been held previous to this time at the residence of Mrs. Trivett. A membership of fifteen reached nearly six times that number before the first year ended. Sunday school was organized upon the opening of the chapel with some twelve or fourteen scholars and there are now over 100 on the roll. A Women's Guild was organized, and has done, and is still doing, valuable service. The young ladies of the congregation

name of the Daughters of the Good Shepherd, and are doing efficient dear service. A striking feature of the service is a vested choir of boys, organized and well trained by T. W. Timberlake. The present members of the executive committee are T. W. Timberlake, president; H. L. Cole, secretary; H. E. Harrington, treasurer; H. F. Huffman, Geo. H. Singer and Thomas E. Foley. Rev. John Haight is now and has been since its organization the rector of the mission.

Zion's Congregation.

The Evangelical Reformed Zion's Congregation is quite young. Rev. Joseph F. Schatz preached his first sermon in the Town Hall in October, 1891. On January 10th, following, the congregation was organized with thirty-eight members. Ground was broken on the 4th of July for the church at the corner of Sherman and Walter avenues, and it was dedicated some months later. The building cost about $8,000. The societies are the Ladies Aid, the Sunday-school, the Choral and the Building Aid. The trustees in 1896 are Fred Wulf, Henry Bardof, George A. Doyas, H. H. Landwehr and August Strumpler. The congregation contemplates the erection of a parsonage. The building committee, aided by several of the trustees, numbered among its members H. W. Kahle, L. Krayvoyzeck, C. Miller, F. Kleine and the pastor. Being a mission the congregation receives from the Board of Home Missions of the Reformed Church $500 annually towards the support of the pastor. Rev. Mr. Schatz says: "The church, standing squarely on the Scriptures as the word of God, is entirely Christian in principle, but for that very reason also purely democratic (in the sense of popular) and liberal in rule and practice. The church practically rules itself without any foreign interference, abiding within the reasonable limits of the constitution. Its gates are wide open to all, its heart is large and warm enough to receive and welcome all who, like those of old, have their delight in the house of God, and obey Him gladly."

St. John's, on the Hill.

Mission Hall witnessed the birth of the youngest congregation of them all, and on March 27, 1892, St. John's

ant Church was planned. A week later Rev. H. Haefner delivered a sermon to a handful of the faithful. Henry Feldman presented the lot on which their brick edifice is built, on the Montgomery pike, half-way up the heights, and during the fall of 1893, the church was dedicated. The structure, with its furnishings, cost about $15,000. Antique oak and yellow pine blend nicely in the finishing. The weather vane on the sextagonal steeple is 173 feet above the floor, and the spire of St. John's is prominent from almost any point in Norwood. Rev. J. Paul Reinhart was the first pastor. Rev. J. B. Erben, the second, was called to the German Protestant Orphan Asylum, in Mt. Auburn and Rev. H. Tessmer is now in charge. The trustees include John Niehaus, Henry Feldman, Philip Voelker, John Hess, Edward Kirk, William Schneder, Casper Goeschel, William Schmidt and George Hathan.

J. U. LLOYD, HARRIS AVENUE

A GRAND FINANCIAL EXHIBIT.

Dorset of figures, while not especially picturesque, are sometimes what the nuts and raisins are to an eight course dinner. No other suburb in the East can make such an exhibit as this series of annual reports which "boiled to the very marrow," shows how Norwood has grown in importance in the short space of five years. The first money which Norwood's treasurer ever handled was a loan of $250 advanced by Edward Mills, to liquidate certain early claims.

The Treasury showed for the year ending March 15, 1890.	
Receipts	$1,673.60
Expenditures	2,031.01
Balance	$1,697.20
Year ending March 31, 1891.	
Receipts	$5,983.84
Expenditures	25,192.87
Balance	726.96
Including 1890 balance	7,417.20
Year ending March 31, 1892.	
Receipts	$11,101.28
Expenditures	10,602.01
Balance	5,432.55
Year ending March 30, 1893.	
Receipts	$37,747.4
Expenditures	31,552.16
Balance	10,755.17
Year ending March 30, 1894.	
Receipts (including balance)	$77,194
Expenditures	39,520.16
Balance	$1,974.18

Is there any other village in Ohio that can show an increase of over eighty times their total of five years? Norwood is not weighed down with any oppressive public debt. The outstanding liabilities at the beginning of 1894 were $149,500, including the water works, village portion of sidewalks, public buildings and general purpose bonds. In addition to these debts there were $394,672.32 worth of 6% bonds in circulation, the principal and

SCHOOL BOARD

A. C. Strobel

Harold Ryland

C. M. Flowers, Sup't

A. P. Hagemeyer

NORWOOD'S SCHOOLS.

A FEW less than a score of years ago the jurist who now occupies the bench in the Probate Court of Hamilton County, was the young pedagogue in charge of the Sharpsburg district school. While Howard Ferris was teaching there he devoted his spare moments to the study of the law, and he abandoned his first love to enter the bar. When named for a judgeship the old Sharpsburg teacher received one of the largest majorities ever given a man in the county, and his re-election was even a greater triumph. Judge Ferris is not the only man identified with Norwood's early school system who has attained distinction. Captain Joseph B. Foraker, twice called to the Governorship of Ohio, once filled the modest but responsible position of school trustee in a district that has become one of the proud boasts of Norwood—a system as nearly perfect as it is possible to be. Prior to 1868 this was a sub-district under the control of the township trustees, but on February 18th of that year, under a new enactment, a call was issued and signed by Moses F. Buxton, Jas. A. McKee, Wm. B. Ferguson, Jas. G. Langdon, John N. Stebern, Wm. M. Langdon, Columbus Williams and Jackson Slane for an election to vote on the establishment of a separate school district. Ten days later the election was held, and Columbus Williams, Jackson Slane and John N. Stebern were chosen members of the first independent board of education of what was afterwards known as the Sharpsburg district, now Norwood special school district Nos. 3 and 17 of Columbia and Mill creek Township. The census at that time showed sixty-one families in the district, with a total population of three hundred and eighteen and a tax duplicate of about $350,000. The building then was a plain, two-story brick structure, on the site of the present central house. One teacher, at a salary of $537.50 per year and a music teacher who drew $75.10 made up "the faculty." The following year, 1869, an extra teacher was employed, but the music item was chopped out. Until 1884 Sharpsburg plodded slowly along and two teachers were sufficient. The present term of 1894 sees fifteen teachers employed in looking after the welfare of Norwood's rising generation.

It was in 1884 that $7,000 were expended for a new four-room building on the pike, but three years later it was again necessary to branch out, and $9,000 were spent in remodeling the building and adding four rooms. The district is a large one, covering three and a half

CHAS. H. WEIDENFELDER.

NORWOOD'S SCHOOLS — The Old and the New.

square miles of territory and in the face of the rapidly increasing population in all directions, it was deemed wise to provide for the primary pupils at centers nearer the extremely distant portions of the district. The Board of Education submitted to the people the proposition to divide the district for primary purposes, and establish branch schools therein. This was approved in March, 1891, by authority to issue $20,000 worth of bonds, which was afterwards increased to $25,000. The district was divided exactly in the middle, good lots were secured near the center of each division, and handsome, substantial brick buildings erected on each lot. The plans were made for four-room buildings, but only two-room, with the halls, were erected at that time. The total cost of that improvement was $25,016.91. These buildings are now full, and under authority granted April 17, 1895, the additions of two rooms to each building have been made, which, with the necessary improvements to the grounds, furniture, heating apparatus, etc., cost $10,000. In 1892, the action of the Platting Commission in straightening Elm street, east of Montgomery pike, left a strip of 17 feet, south of school house, which was leased by the Board of Education, with privilege of purchase for $2,500. This carried with it the title to school house, 20 feet wide which has since been vacated, thus adding $7,830 feet to the central school lot, and making that lot 167 feet wide by an average depth of about 340 feet, and worth with the improvements, about $35,000. The retiring board included: President A. Comstock, Harold Bylindant, A. P. Housemeyer. During their term an unfeeling controversy arose. W. S. Cadman and Chas. H. Weisenshiker, declaring that discrimination had been made against the central ward. The people elected a bond issue to increase the membership to six. A. C. S. was held about April, 1894, and at that election Harold Bylindant, Jno. P. Zimmermann, L. R. Edwards, Chas. H. Weisenshiker and A. P. Housemeyer were chosen. Mr. H. was elected president, and Mr. Zimmermann, treasurer. Prof. C. M. Thorne has been the principal of the central part, which had charge of the... the grades, has been assisted by Miss Josephine B. Sheldon, Mrs. Carrie A. Hunt, Lizzie A. Louw, Jno. A. B. Beebe, Miss Louw, Leonardtoner, Louw... ner, Jno. E. Byers, Miss Low ler, Lena Martin, Hunt Booker Huszt Annette, Louw Bole, and Mrs. Bill C. Linwon.

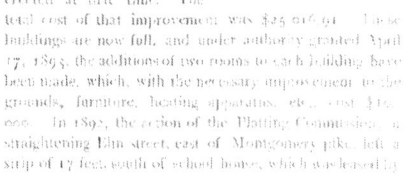

THE REALM OF MELODY.

IN a musical way, Norwood takes rank above that attained by many cities of greater pretensions. When the South Norwood Musical and Literary Society was in the midst of its successful social reign a few years ago, no one could foresee that some occasional instrumental contributions to the programmes prefaced the organization of such an institution as the Norwood Orchestra. There were just six gentlemen who first met in October, 1889, and two months later they made their orchestral debut. G. W. Gale was the chosen leader of the musical pilgrims who, during the spring of 1890, gave their first series of concerts, a feature that has since been an accepted part of the winter life of Norwood's artistic folk. At that time the membership had been trebled, and a piano was added to the possessions of the orchestra. Max Grau conducted some of the full rehearsals in 1891, but Mr. Gale again wielded the baton during the second successful series of concerts. Prof. William A. Kuckel, once one of Gilmore's cornet soloists, now directs the orchestra, filling the rôle of instructor as well. The brilliant success of the past years was repeated during the musical seasons of 1892 and 1893. Since the inauguration of those winter concerts Miss Laura Wyeler, Mrs. Lucy S. Hudson, Miss George Myers, Miss Mae Betscher, Edwin J. Walther, Herman Bellstedt, William A. Heinrich, A. E. Masik, John Ruedhe and T. J. Sullivan have appeared as soloists for the orchestra, inasmuch as "Norwood deserves the best."

George Fischer is president of the orchestra, A. C. Sanders, vice-president; Harold Ryson, secretary, and Walther M. Davis, treasurer. Here are the members and

A. Y. REID PARK AVENUE.

stolius, George Puchta, Chas. H. Gegreve and Ferd. Bassier, 2nd violins, Harold Ryland, John L. Vinc and Chas. Stratenhaver. Viola, A. H. Pape; Cello, A. C. Strobel; Bass, Frank Seebach. Flute, G. V. Hattersley; Clarionet, I. H. Schmidt, 1st cornet, H. A. Pugh; 2nd cornet, J. G. Evans; French horns, H. E. Knauff and M. Koob; trombone, W. M. Davis, and drums, A. McEnair.

The Norwood Choral Society is an organization that, during its brief existence, has promised well. There are now over thirty voices enrolled. G. P. Evans is the director of the society, and the accompanists are Miss Josephine Davison, piano, and Miss Bartha Estep, organ. Dr. N. L. Scott is president and George H. Singer, secretary and treasurer. Upon the executive board with Director Evans are Thomas B. Estep and H. L. Harrington. The Choral Society covers the vocal field as thoroughly and artistically as the orchestra does the instrumental.

West Norwood numbers among its institutions the Cornet and Reed Band and instructed by Henry Klenz, the members have long made their presence known. In

new uniforms they make a splendid appearance, and there is no telling how many budding Gilmores may be in the ranks of these faithful members. John W. Hall, president and manager; B. R. Hall, Dallas Hall, William Cordes, Louis Cordes, Joseph Mersch, John Cordes, Edward Cook, Edward S. Ross, Earl Robertson and Claude Menyon

The Field of Sport.

RECRUITS to the ranks of the cyclists are multiplying rapidly, and with the completion of the boulevard, Norwood will be a great magnet for the riders of the steeds of steel. The Norwood Wheelmen, organized during March, 1894, with W. S. Gwynn, president, John Douglass, secretary and treasurer; Clarence Evans, captain; Walter Stewart, lieutenant; W. C. Hattersley, John Franklin and Robert E. Edmondson, board of governors. There are enough ladies who ride the cycle to form a club of their own, if they so elected. There are plans afoot

the youth of the village can turn out as many ball players as any other town of its size. There are several teams among the young swatters of the pigskin. Norwood had a berth in the old Highland League a few years ago, and the Norwoods of 1893, managed by "Phil" Cross, created something of a stir in the world of amateur base ball players. There is a regiment of the genus "fans" in the borough, and "Norwood Day," a festival at League Park in compliment to Ashley Lloyd, the treasurer of the Cincinnati Base Ball Club—a Norwood man—was a novel event, in 1893, that created no little comment all through the circuit. There is no other village in the State that can surpass Norwood in its rural possessions and advantages for out-of-door

LODGE ROOM SECRETS.

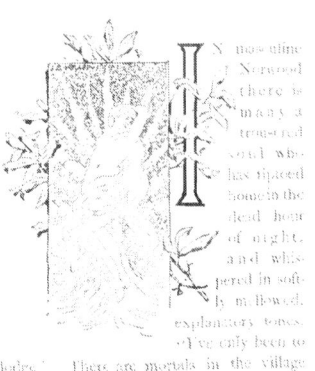

IN nowadays of Norwood there is many a trusted soul who has sipped home in the dead hour of night, and whispered in softly mellowed explanatory tones: "I've only been to lodge." There are mortals in the village who have trodden the heated sands of the desert in the marches of the Syrian Nobles of the Mystic Shrine. There are Masons who have never ventured beyond the mysteries of the blue lodge and others who have not stopped this side 32° in the Scottish Rite. You can find Knights Templar, Knights of Pythias, Odd Fellows, Grand Army men—in fact, representatives of almost every secret order extant, and when it comes down to royalty there are Princes of the Orient in numbers sufficient to fill all the spare rooms in Windsor Castle,

W. S. GWYNN.

if the Queen ever felt lonesome and yearned for blue-blooded company. Although Norwood has no body of Free and Accepted Masons, she is the bone and sinew of Pleasant Ridge lodge, and contributes largely in officering that organization.

The Knights of Pythias were first of the secret orders to gain foothold in Norwood, and August 15, 1888, with twenty-nine charter members, Cowan Lodge, No. 304, was instituted by P. C. Dr. W. G. Herr, of Mistletoe Lodge at Madisonville. William Loser was the father of the lodge and first Past Chancellor. Those who have "passed through the chairs" since that time and now wear the jewel of Master of Work are W. S. Cadman, W. G. Beitz, C. E. Gegrave, Geo. Enlor, Henry Hoffaran, A. S. Hoffaran, John P. Zimmerman, Jr., J. E. Zimmerman, W. W. Russell and Frank J. McHugh. From quarters in the town hall Cowan Lodge soon moved into a cozy home of its own, at the corner of Montgomery pike and Harris avenue. Cowan is one of the "rival" lodges of Ohio, and the Knights have given a series of entertainments that have been features of Norwood's social life. The officers are H. P. Smith, C. C.; Chas. J. McQuerty, V. C.; John E. Vine, Prelate; Dr. J. C. Cadwallader, M. of A.; L. R. Edwards, I. G.; John Butler, O. G.; J. P. Zimmerman, Jr., M. of E.; Chas. H. Westenfelder, M. of F.; T. W. Hoffman, K. of R. and S.; W. S. Cadman, W. W. Russell and J. P. Zimmerman, Jr., trustees.

The Royal Arcanum is represented by Norwood Council, No. 1331, which was instituted January 3, 1891, by Deputy Grand Regent Edward Buck, assisted by Deputy Supreme Regent W. J. Lowers. There were just

J. M. HOOPER, CROWN STREET.

two dozen charter members who had been recruited largely by Winfield S. Gwynn. That gentleman was chosen Regent. The Royal Arcanum's growth has been slow, but a net gain shows that the council is moving in the right direction. The present officers are: Past Regent, Harold Ryland; Regent, William S. Cadman; Vice-Regent, Dr. John J. Winn; Orator, John J. Hoover; Guide, Lewis H. Gebhart; Chaplain, George W. Stacey; Warden, Joseph Lammers; Sentry, Ernest Dietz; Secretary, Winfield S. Gwynn; Collector, Chas. H. Weisenfelder; Treasurer, Jacob G. Graf; Trustees, John Franklin, Harold Ryland and William S. Cadman.

The National Union is represented in the borough by Norwood Council, No. 488, which was instituted with forty-nine charter members April 10, 1891. They, too, meet at Pythian Hall, and present roll of officers include: President, P. S. Bettinger; Ex-President, Geo. Encke; Secretary, Geo. H. Hinderman; Financial Secretary, W. J. Carey; Treasurer, A. E. Lowry; Speaker, F. A. Zimmermann; Chaplain and Medical Examiner, Dr. J. C. Cadwallader, and Usher, Chas. Kerner.

SAMUEL F. HARRIS, HARRIS AVENUE AND DEEP CREEK ROAD.

MACK, THE DOG PAPER CARRIER.

There is one pretty smart resident of East Norwood whose name is not in the directory. "Mack" is a regular boarder at the Hoffman Lower-house, and he is one of the most remarkable members of the borough's canine contingent. Mack is a water spaniel, and while he was a pup he was trained in the way that all good dogs should be.

"Mack's" education was not considered finished until he was taught to run down to the front porch every morning, take the paper and carry it into the house. "Mack" was an apt pupil, and made a successful news agent, but he was too ambitious. After he had completed the task regularly assigned to him, "Mack" got into the habit of skirmishing around the neighborhood and collecting all the newspapers in sight, until the Lower Hoffman house resembled a distributing agency. It was easy enough to teach "Mack" to be a paper carrier, but it took several years to break him of a habit that for a time created an impression that East Norwood sheltered one of those pests—the man who gets openly and odorously somebody else's newspaper

Bird's-eye View of Norwood from George A. Turrell's Subdivision

TWO BRIGADES OF FIRE FIGHTERS.

THREE days after the home of P. J. Schneider was burned to the ground — March 9th, 1889 — the West Norwood Volunteer Fire Brigade took the field. While the ruins of that house were smoldering, a subscription list was passed around and the nucleus of the fund to equip the fire fighters thus recruited. The original membership roll of twenty-five has been doubled, and the brigade continues its valued services as a stock company. The shares are but $1.00, and the dues $1.00 a year. To the original building on Mills avenue, two additions were made. The village provided a good engine and hose reel. The ladder wagon was made by "the boys," for in the ranks are carpenters and blacksmiths. West Norwood's ladies presented both a bell and a flag to the brigade. Although out of the bailiwick the brigade distinguished itself at the St. Aloysius Asylum conflagration. Early on the morning of March 6th, 1894, there was an alarm given and West Norwood brigade turned out only to witness their own headquarters in flames. The origin of the fire was a mystery, and, notwithstanding the Aaron McNeill only watched the approach of the fire, hose and engine, hose and ladder were all licked up. The loss was $1,500, and the committees on rebuilding got to work at once. Upon the site of the destroyed engine house a two-story pressed brick edifice will prove the handsomest home the brigade ever claimed. The second floor will be converted into a hall. Contracts for the reconstruction were let the last week in March and the work commenced at once. The officers during the late administration were: President, Joseph H. Lamont; Vice-President, Edward R. Hall; Secretary, Chas. H. Wyckoff; and Trea-

NORWOOD VOLUNTEER FIRE CO., N. J.

MEMBERS WEST NORWOOD VOLUNTEER FIRE BRIGADE.

ees William Jannings, Trustees, Frank Ronnebaum and Henry Jaeger Jr.; Chief, Wm Dancer; Lieutenants, John W. Hall, Chas. Woerz, Oliver Devoe and Charles Bohnlid.

A blaze that wiped out several houses on the pike above Harris avenue led to the organization of Norwood Volunteer Fire Company, which is located in a cozy engine house on the main thoroughfare, below the bridge. They are well equipped for battling with the flames. F. J. McFarlin, President, Dr. C. W. Tuthill, Vice President; W. G. Berry, Secretary and W. M. Langdon, Treasurer, are on the executive roster. The Chief is Philip Voelker, and John W. Tidball is his assistant. Thomas Morgan and Dr. J. P. Hastings are the lieutenants and Charles Anderson Custodian of the engine house. The members are divided into three companies, viz: Hose, Dr. W. H. Hopkins, Captain; Richard Dellarm, Assistant Captain; John Hercksall, William Hercksall, Ben Eich and William Hummell. Engine, Henry Gaee, Captain; Gus Seavy, Assistant Captain; George Higene, George Halsman, Harry Price, William Higene and August Hinderman. Hook and Ladder, Edward Wiggeringler, Captain; John Singh, Assistant Captain; Edward Stoat, Philip Bierman, John Gloss, William Ellington and Charles Waite. The water works, with the fire plugs so well distributed about town, affords Norwood much greater protection than ever than it ever before enjoyed.

TOUR OF THE PEOPLE'S BANKS.

Where there is thrift you find "the people's bank," building associations. There are four in Norwood. The Norwood is the pioneer, antedating in abundance back to November 14, 1882. For years Col. E. P. Luse was its president. To the present roster of officers is credited

Directors: H. W. Kuhls, John L. Vine, J. H. Brachmann, A. N. Siebern, J. E. Metz, and T. H. Ringgold.

The Norwood Improved was the second building and loan company to invade the growing field, and it brought push and enterprise with it. Chas. L. Page is President; D. G. Zoller, Vice President; E. A. Zimmerman, Secretary; A. P. Hagemeyer, Treasurer; Directors, Walter Carey, E. E. Van Ausdo, Hugo E. Knauft, A. B. Hollis, Theodore Trimble, F. J. McFarlan and W. G. Williams. Semi-annual dividends are paid and weekly meetings held in the Hopkins Avenue depot, a structure by the way that was built and is owned by residents of South Norwood.

The Elsmere Building and Loan Company was incorporated in July, 1896, by E. J. Morton, H. P. Hathaway, W. J. Collins, Geo. F. Cook, Edwin McMillen, A. W. Eastman, A. A. Brown, Wm. Kerentz, Wm. Thorburn, H. Ensign and A. Mallo &c. The officers are David Davis, President; F. G. Triman, Vice President; E. J. Morton, Treasurer; Ferd Fromler, Secretary; G. A. Willard and H. P. Hathaway, Finance Committee.

The West Norwood Building and Loan Association is officered by Dr. J. J. Winn, President; Chas. H. Weisenfelder, Vice President; Peter L. Schneider, Secretary; L. H. Gebhart, Assistant Secretary; Gustav Schmidt, Treasurer, and Benj. Overmohl, Fred Schmidt, Wm. Jannings, Oliver Devoe, Joseph Espel, John Kolsent, H. Jostwerth, H. Rikhoff, and Fred Dan-

SOCIAL WHISPERS.

Norwood is no
longer a town. Nor-
wood as it
has existed
from a lit-
erary stand-
point for
a year,
and that was
when the Lowell
Literary Society annually celebrated the birthday of the father of his Country. "The Lowell" has
passed away and its library was willed to
the school. The social life of Norwood
plays no inconsiderable part in its history.
The Chautauquans have had a successful
career. There are several reading, euchre
and whist clubs, while incidents of the ball
have been features of the winter programme. The Soro-
sis Club is composed solely of young ladies, and is officered
by Miss Etta Hill, president, Miss Ida Bosse, vice-president, Miss Carolyn Tuttell, secretary, and Miss Gr...
Reynolds, treasurer. The Physical Culture Club, instructed by Miss Carrie Goldsmith, meets in the late afternoon.

JOHN P. ...

zations, with Mrs. J. A. Knapp,
president; Mrs. J. U. Lloyd,
vice-president; Mrs. Ren Mulford, Jr., secretary, and Mrs.
H. C. Meader, treasurer.
The Entre Nous Literary Society is made up of young
folks who recently essayed
amateur theatricals. The officers are W. G. Bertoli,
president; Miss Josie Jackson, vice-president; D. E.
Woolley, secretary; Miss Dai-
sy Ross, treasurer; Harry R.
Frick, censor, and Miss Lot-
tie Tudor, editor of the Budget.
The younger devotees of Terp-
sichore pay court to the
goddess of the dance at the
"cosmos cotillons," of the
Comus Club, which claims
as its members, W. G. Bertoli, president; Fred Mc-
Queeny, vice-president; George A. Sawyer, secretary and
treasurer; John Barker, Joe Barker, James Berry, Bush
Parker, Walter Stewart and Harry King.

Tennis is one of the most popular pastimes of the
summer. The Ideal Park Club has its courts on Forest
avenue, and the Norwood Club's grounds are on Beech
street, in East Norwood.
There are several private
courts where the knights and
ladies of the racquet love to
congregate. Fred McQueeny
is president of the Ideal Park
Club; Charles Charles, vice-
president; George A. Saw-
yer, secretary; Harry R.
Frick, treasurer, and Will G.
Bertoli, superior. The Norwood Tennis Club's officers
are President, Harry C. Hes-
...Vice-President, O. P. Cobb;
Secretary, Miss Minnie Mc-
Geehin; Treasurer, George
H. Singer; Executive Board,
A. W. Hoffman, W. G. Betts,
F. C. Paige, A. H. Si...
and Ren Mulford, Jr. The
...Tennis Club, with
courts on ...street, is the
finest in the field. A. L. Brown
is President and superviser;
Elinor Bosse, Secretary, and
...

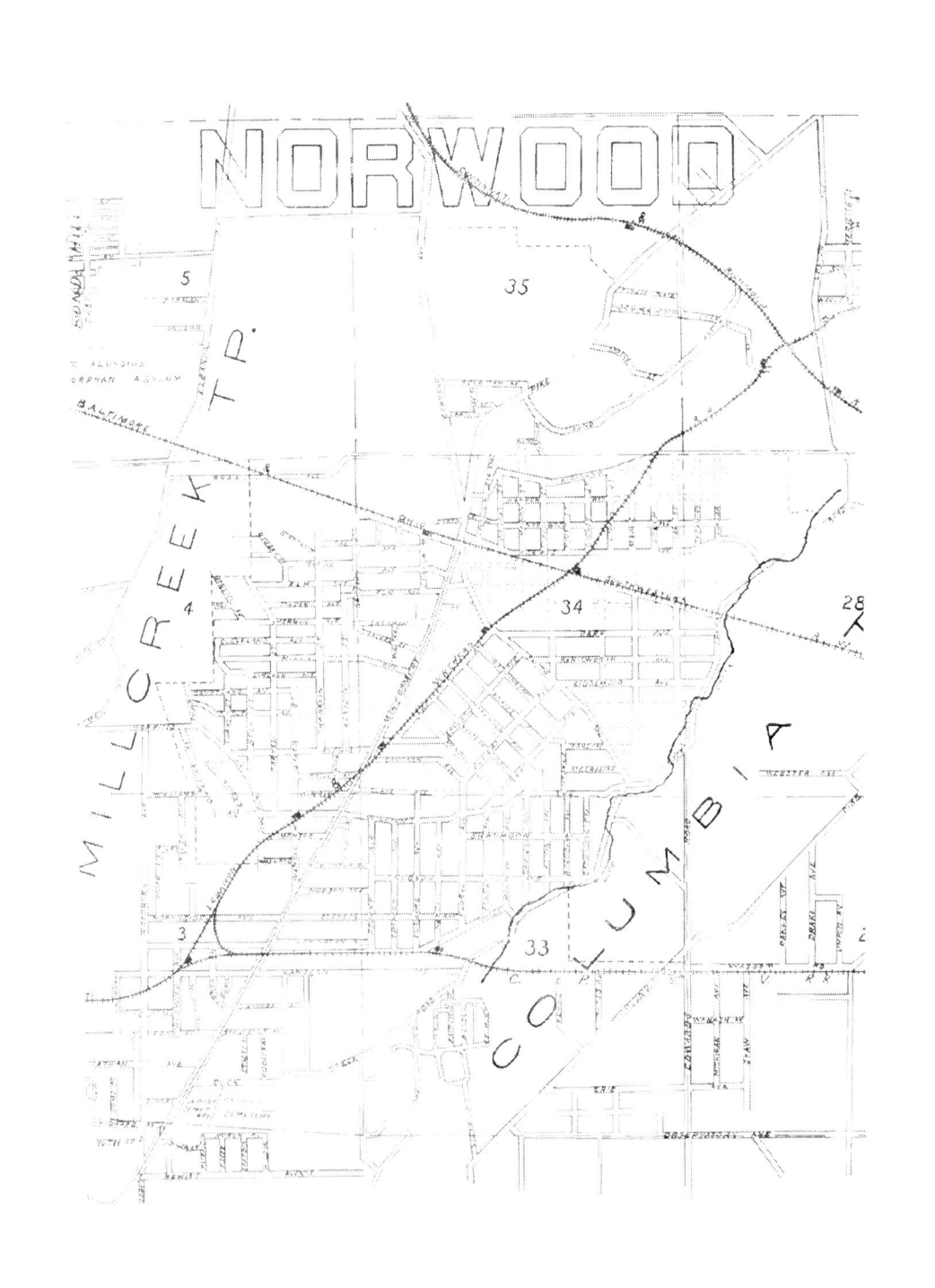

NORWOOD

NORWOOD'S PEOPLE.

THE intense personal interest that the majority of her people take in the welfare of Norwood is doubtless responsible for the commanding position she holds among the suburbs to-day. It was at Columbus, before a meeting of a legislative committee, that Judge John P. Murphy, a resident of Bond Hill, eloquently referred to Norwood as "the Chicago of Hamilton County." Among Norwood's 6,000 people to-day there are men in all walks of life, some prominent in city and state, and some whose fame is international. Louis T. Rebisso, the sculptor, is one of these—the artist who gave to Washington her statue of General J. B. McPherson, to Chicago, the grand tribute to U. S. Grant, that adorns Lincoln Park, and whose statue of General William Henry Harrison will be one of Cincinnati's art treasures, is one of Norwood's citizens. There are merchants, wholesale and retail; attorneys, real estate men, insurance men, railroaders, contractors, commercial tourists, newspaper people, teachers—in fact almost every department in life's busy hive is represented in Norwood's happy family, and the great majority of them own their homes. The American Pharmaceutical Association came to Norwood for its president, and Prof. J. U. Lloyd has occupied that position not only once but twice. He was first called to that post of honor in 1886, and in 1891 the summons was repeated. Prof. Lloyd has an international reputation, and is one of the most eminent scientists in the world. He has extensively contributed to the literature of his profession, and has made discoveries that have worked revolutions in the school of medicine. One of his works, "The Chemistry of Medicines," is an accepted textbook in many medical colleges, and with his brother, C. G. Lloyd, a botanist of note, he is now completing an exhaustive volume on "The Drugs and Medicines of North America." He has for years occupied the chair of Chemistry in the Eclectic Medical Institute and that of Pharmacy in the Cincinnati College of Pharmacy.

LOUIS T. REBISSO

DR. JOHN WEYER

"Eighty Distinguished Pharmacists of the World" is the title of a volume recently published at Geneva, Switzerland, and John Uri Lloyd was one of three Americans whose life work was recorded within its pages. Alexander Fries, head of the chemical firm of Alex. Fries & Bros., is another resident who has gained fame abroad, as well as success at home. He is a descendant of a long line of professors of mathematics, and was born in Germany. Mr. Fries spent twelve years of his early life in Spain, devoting most of his time towards developing the country traversed by the Sierra Morenas. His efforts were crowned with such success as to warrant the Spanish Government's official recognition by elevating him to Knighthood, and bestowing upon him the high order of Carlos III., an honor heretofore attained by but few foreigners. Dr. John Weyer, who was Norwood's first mayor, was once president of the Ohio State Pharmaceutical Board, as well as president of the Cincinnati College of Pharmacy. He was the projector and is the president of the Retail Druggists' Insurance Association, which at once found and filled a field of usefulness. R. P. Bellsmith, whose camera has played no little part in the preparation of this work, is "one of the people." The Photographers' Association of Ohio elected him president, and at the World's Fair in Chicago, the blue ribbon of a first prize winner was draped over the exhibit of this Norwood fotografer. The Western Union Telegraph Company is represented in the persons of Manager Charles E. Page and Cashier Allen B. Clark, while several attachés also help to swell Norwood's census. V. H. Singer, the agent of the United States Express Company, and Preston K. Kuhn, recently installed as General Superintendent of that company, at Cincinnati, give the "transportation department" a good standing in the roll call of vocations. The disciples of Blackstone who dwell within Norwood's gates, include A. McNeill, O. P. Uebi, W. G. Williams, David Davis, Edward Moulinier, C. E. Prior and A. A. Brown. The latter founded "The Lumber Worker" and has been editor of "The Furniture Worker" for ten years past. The fraternity of railroad men has several bright representatives, including C. C. Ryan, the General Passenger Agent of the Chesapeake and Ohio; Charles Patton, the Pinmaster, and Frank Zimmerman, General Passenger Agent, of the Queen and Crescent; and H. E. Sowyer, Master of Transportation of the C. L. and N.; George H. Singer, of the B. & O. S. W., doubtless possesses one of the finest collections of rare etchings, artists' proofs in the West. Good libraries are numerous, evidence that the literary tastes of Norwood's people are good. Samuel T. Harris, one of the pioneers of the borough, has a magnificent collection of valuable tomes. He is an ardent lover of horse flesh, an owner of fine stock, and his writings have been of such a nature, that in the trotting world he is accepted as an authority upon the horse. It is a singular coincidence that the editors of both Cincinnati Catholic weekly newspapers reside at Norwood—Joseph Schoenberger, of the Catholic Telegraph, and Bruno Ritter, of Die Wahrheitsfreund. Hugo E. Knauff, L. E. Van Ausdel, John Findlay, Richard Hempel and C. L. Cist are recruits from the banking districts. William J. O'Neill, of the Board of Elections, is one of the "new comers." Rev. J. A. Markham, who is pastor of the Bethel, that great mission on the river front, claims Norwood for his home, and Rev. A. J. Reynolds, one of the veterans of the Presbyterian church, resides on South avenue. Rev. T. J. Harris and Rev. J. R. Powell are other resident ministers. J. A. Knapp, another contributor to the beauty of this work, upholds the dignity of the artists. It is meet perhaps to observe that H. F. Farny painted several of his celebrated Indian pictures while he made his home under the stroke wind "on the heights." Four ex-members of the State House of Representatives are "at home" here: W. M. Day, Chas. Irline, W. H. Decker and Sh. Keer. The First Regiment O. N. G. contains several officers inside Norwood's territory, including Major W. M. Day, Major Ed Lovett, Captain W. J. O'Neill, Jr., Captain Sam Kennedy and Lieutenant C. Davidson, of Company E. Dr. A. W. Elliott attended as Surgeon Light Artillery, O. N. G., for services in the Norwood connection. Residents not in the men are

SAMUEL T. HARRIS

numerous, for many of them have emphasized their belief in the virtue of their own arguments by building themselves in the "Gem of the Highlands." John G. Leatherton, of the Elsmere Syndicate; Robert Leslie, Philip Moessinger, J. W. Fritsch, W. H. Dicks, the Bockers; Henry Feldman, Harry O. Cleneay and S. P. Lane are only a few of those on the roster. "Uncle Bob" Leslie has always been active in the development of the borough. Floral avenue, the handsome thoroughfare which runs from Norwood Park through Elsmere, was his pet project, and when it was built (the great avenue in South Norwood) a tribute was paid to its genius. E. C. Peuge and Henry C. Meader are prominent members of the family of ticket brokers, and both travel as far as East Norwood every day. They are known all over the land. Among pedagogues there are W. S. Colman, former superintendent of Norwood's schools, now at Ludlow Grove; H. H. Bruder, of Woodward High School, and Prof. J. C. Kinney. There is a veritable hive of shoe men in South Norwood, including H. M. Richardson, George T. Hipple, C. C. Robinson, A. A. King and Wm. Hirsch, while B. Albers resides in the west borough. Harry M. Lane, the mechanical engineer; Chas. H. Gingreve, Secretary of the Wholesale Grocer's Association of Cincinnati; John B. Maas, of Fraxel & Maas; Fred Witte, of the Moerlein Brewing Co.; S. B. Markland, who has been Grand Marshal of the Grand Chapter of Royal Arch Masons for six years; Seth Hayes, the Director of the Cincinnati Society of Natural History; A. S. Reed, H. L. Harrington, with Ault & Wiborg; W. E. Kreidler, Secretary of Superintendent J. M. Dawson, of the John Shillito Company; S. S. Kingery, of the Kingery Manufacturing Company; W. C. Hatersley, of the Victor Safe Company; B. C. Smith, of the Cincinnati Suspender Company; T. J. McFarlan, of the Dexter Lumber Company; C. F. Seaman, who is President of the Union of A. P. S. C.; Jas. A. C. Cutrell; F. W. Jewell, of the Union Central Life Insurance Company; W. C. Brown, of the Cleveland Rubber Company; Wallace M. Davis, Superintendent of the Cincinnati Omnibus Company; W. J. Winterbottom, Superintendent of the Cincinnati Transfer Company; W. S.

J. W. AYRES

Johnson, the insurance man; Peter Brooks, the fruit dealer; Wesley A. Stewart, the chemist; H. J. Reedy,

ELSMERE

EAST NORWOOD

ELSMERE, C. P. & V. R. R., Hopkins Ave., C. L. & N. Ry. EAST NORWOOD, C. & O. S. W. Ry.

elevator manufacturer; Julius Fricke, of the J. Wilder Co.; W. J. Radliff, of Keens and Paffel Chemical Co.; E. H. Rudesch, the inventor; since George Stone, with the A. E. Burkhardt Co.; Lytle Sweeney, of the faculty of the Unined school; Charles W. Evans, the — and — tax factor; those are but few of the Cincinnati men who, during the present Norwood in the morning, transact and resettle. In dilute the villages in Hamilton's the trading home of Albert Mohbach, part of whose place hes in Norwood. A. C. Rusch, head of the old renowned firm of Rusch, Mason & Co., now the United States Printing Company, is the nearest neighbor of this man Democratist. He is a great cycler, of Louis Walton, one of the Emerys' cities, and an enthusiast on whist. The

Mrs. Helen J. Bowler hold the next set in South Norwood, now occupied by Charles E. Stone and wife, no Corn Ave.

C. L. Hauser, however, was the pioneer of the first section, taking possession of his new home in the Bauck e moved in. While Norwood has its usual men of note, there are also among Norwood's new-come who have distinction. Mrs. E. C. Trivers a painter of ability the foremost of the decorative artists of the

The Women's Building at the World's Fair contains a number of her works, and the Arkansas Building, decorated by her. Several bras here and in other cities have been decorated by her. In art store Mrs. S.

A. W. MAUSED

W. Lloyd has been a prolific contributor, and some of her poems are gems. Many a house, beautiful in the borough, is replete with tributes to the artistic tastes of the reigning goddess of the home.

A STUDY IN WILD FLOWERS.

Norwood's future seems superlatively bright. Five years ago the most enthusiastic dreamer in the borough could not foresee the glorious tableau of to-day. The trend of progress is toward the hills and the rich valleys of old Columbia. As the grand settlement of homes increases, the sylvan spots, so much reminiscent of the country, will grow fewer. Some of them should be spared for our children, and our children's children. Among all of Norwood's auxiliaries there is no Park Board, and an immediate mission for one. Some years ago the suggestion was made to preserve the strip of woodland between the Baltimore and Ohio Southwestern and H— avenue, just east of Forest avenue. It was a good idea then. It is a better one now. Perhaps in all of Norwood there is no wilder spot then than narrow tract. It is all hills and hollows, with here and there a few latter h— vionets of the forest and the most modest wild flowers thrive there together. The beech, the walnut, the hickory, the locust, the sycamore, the poplar, and the buckeye are among the living delegates in that congregation of trees. Before Jack Frost has fairly been driven off the earth, Queen Flora's reign commences in that favored spot. The spring beauties, with their delicate blossoms, are among the first. Then comes the violet, here blue as the azure heavens above, and there, white as a bit of porcelain. Dog-tooth lilies, with their gray striped petals, come early and go early. The heart shaped

strange contrast. In the shadiest spots rock moss abounds, its blossoms looking like a flowery Pleiades in a bed of malachite. The snowy bloom of the blood root is one of the prettiest of the treasures of the woods. The dog wood and red bud proudly contribute their share to the welcome of Spring. Later on the umbrella shaped May apple takes its place in the procession with its waxy flowers whose lemon tinted heart gives forth a sickening aroma. "Pepper and salt," the larkspur, the ground ivy with its tiny blue-eyed blossoms, not much larger than a pin head, the fragrant wild lilac — all these and more are the trophies that are to be gathered in a jaunt through this beautiful woodland spot. Ferns are plentiful, and when the autumn comes, the golden rod and purple aster become there. Norwood is young. No Springer or no West has yet appeared to make his name a benefaction that would ring through all the ages. Serpentine avenue is plowed through this bit of forest, but it seems cleared a sacrilege to despoil the place. It should be kept as a playground for the children of tomorrow and the day after. If public opinion is favorable too surely a way, steps might be taken to acquire it by lease or purchase. The Norwood of the future would rise up and call the Norwood of the present blessed, if that beautiful spot were dedicated as "Norwood Park," to the people and their heirs forever.

Two Presidents.

UNCLE SAM has had his eye on Norwood, and while the United States has not yet called any of her citizens to jump into the administrative band wagon and handle the reins, half a dozen or more organizations of national importance have honored her citizens. For the third time in its history the American Ticket Brokers Association, at its meeting in Washington, in May, 1894, elected Henry C. Meade, as president. The G. E. and I. W. D. A., while being interpreted means the Ohio, Kentucky and Indiana Wholesale Druggists Association, also elected a Norwood man to preside over its deliberations — N. Ashley Lloyd.

THE COLD WATER TRIUMVIR.

THE Trustees of the Water Works are prominent in business circles in Cincinnati. Dr. Alfred Springer, after finishing his education in the Public Schools, went to the University of Heidelberg, Germany, where he enjoyed the advantages of studying under the celebrated Professors Bunsen, Kirchhoff, Erlenmeyer, Arnold, and Kuhne. In his eighteenth year he graduated with high honors, taking the degrees Ph. D. and A. M. In 1873, Dr. Springer returned to Cincinnati, associating himself with Alex. Lyles & Bros. In 1887, he was elected corresponding member of The British Association for Advancement of Science—an honor he still retains. In 1892, he was elected Vice-President of the American Association for Advancement of Science, and Chairman of the Chemical Section. Dr. Springer has been President of the Cincinnati Chemical Society. His principal contributions to science are: The Discovery of the Nitrate Ferments in Decaying Plants, Dynamic Equilibrium in Forces Swinging in Opposite Arcs, High Centered Gravity to Overcome Frictional Resistance, and the Absence of Higher per Inharmonic Particles in Aluminum. He has received over thirty patents for his inventions, including an aluminum violin. In October 1891, the doctor moved to Norwood, and he has taken an active interest in all matters pertaining to the welfare of this growing suburb.

George Puchta is a grand specimen of a self-made man. He is a Cincinnati boy, and from his youth he has thrived on hard work. In 1851, he entered the employ of Post & Co. as book-keeper, and nine years later he was the head of the house, acquiring

busine , and with E. N. Paul as his associate, the Queen City Supply Company entered upon a career that has been phenomenally successful. Mr. Puchta brought lots of energy into the board.

Henry Rikhoff, who served during the short and was then re-elected for the long term, is one of Cincinnati's best known furniture men. He is the head of the firm of H. Rikhoff & Co., is president of the Cincinnati Furniture Manufacturers' Association and third vice-president of the National Furniture Manufacturers' Association, and in 1892 served as secretary and treasurer of the latter. He left his native place, Covington, for Norwood, some years ago, and while residing across the bridge was the first treasurer of the Kentucky Council, C. K. of A. Mr. Rikhoff was one of the moving spirits in the Furniture Expositions at Music Hall.

The water works triumvir never held public office before, but no veterans ever made a better showing than they have done.

A FEW PERSONAL REMARKS.

When, by an emphatic vote, Norwood declared in favor of a water works system, he elected some eminent and distinguished citymen went before council and asked that this work be accorded official recognition, and their communication met with favor. By resolution, endorsed by Mr. Thomson, council named Ben Mullins, Edward Werner G. F. to historians of the village and set forth in writing this official mode a part of the water works record. The gentlemen who made it possible for the work to gain such endorsement were H. C. Meader, C. F. Pope, R. P. Bedinoth, Robert Leash & Co., Moessinger, Fritsch & Hogle, J. C. Floyd, M. O. Springer, E. D. Baker, A. McNeill, E. McLeod, Wm. Windhorst, Henry Rikhoff, N. Ashley, David Wallace, M. Davis, E. W. Jewel, George Phillips, A. C. Strick, W. W. Russell, H. J. Roth and A. V. Beall. In the preparation of this address, words of encouragement, backed by deeds were numerous. No others have ever attempted a work of such magnitude, and so thorough; there were men concerned who were putting up capital, their own as well as the change prices at the bank. It would not be possible for all Norwood's membership

for there are many others who how it is, and who have lent materially to the history, growth and development of Norwood, but those whose names are emblazoned on the advertising pages have emphasized their interest in Norwood, her homes and her people.

MARSHAL KEHOE'S REIGN.

Back in the old days when Norwood's souls numbered as many hundreds as they now do thousand, Gerald Kehoe was the village man of all work. Many was the role he filled during a week, and he starred in everything, from a landscape gardener to a gentleman who shoveled coal. When Norwood donned her first robes as a municipal body, Gerald Kehoe was called into service as town marshal. Many are the stories told of his career in that office, and one of the best dates back to one Fourth of July. That morning, while Mayor Al-

C. R. Edwards

Nor— was quietly celebrating the Nation's birthday. Marshal Kehoe made his appearance, and informed his honor of a threatened raid of shell workers.

"There be a lot of 'em coming out this afternoon," declared the marshal, "and I think I'll nabe four extra policemen."

And so the mayor indorsed the plan for more protection, making the stipulation that the Marshal swear them in. Gathering the quartet of his chosen followers together, Marshal Kehoe marched them to the town hall, where Clerk Wichger happened to be at the moment. Arming his recruits with clubs, Marshal Kehoe got them in line, and proceeded to administer the oath of office.

"Hold up your right hands," he commanded. (Four arms of assorted sizes were raised in the air.) "Do yez solemnly swear," continued the marshal, "to support the constitution of the United States and the constitution of the State of Ohio." At this point he got off the constitutional track. But after a moment's pause, he concluded, in triumphant tones, "and do yez promis to serve the village of Norwood, as policemen, as you would here God?"

The newly pledged officers swung their clubs all that day, but the shell workers changed their route and did not go through Norwood.

Norwood's Home Market.

While nearly every store of prominence in Cincinnati caters to Norwood, by running out special delivery wagons, the borough is well supplied with home talent. There are half a dozen groceries, several butchers, daily markets, three drug stores, tailor shops, bakeries, dry goods stores and candy shops. There are also

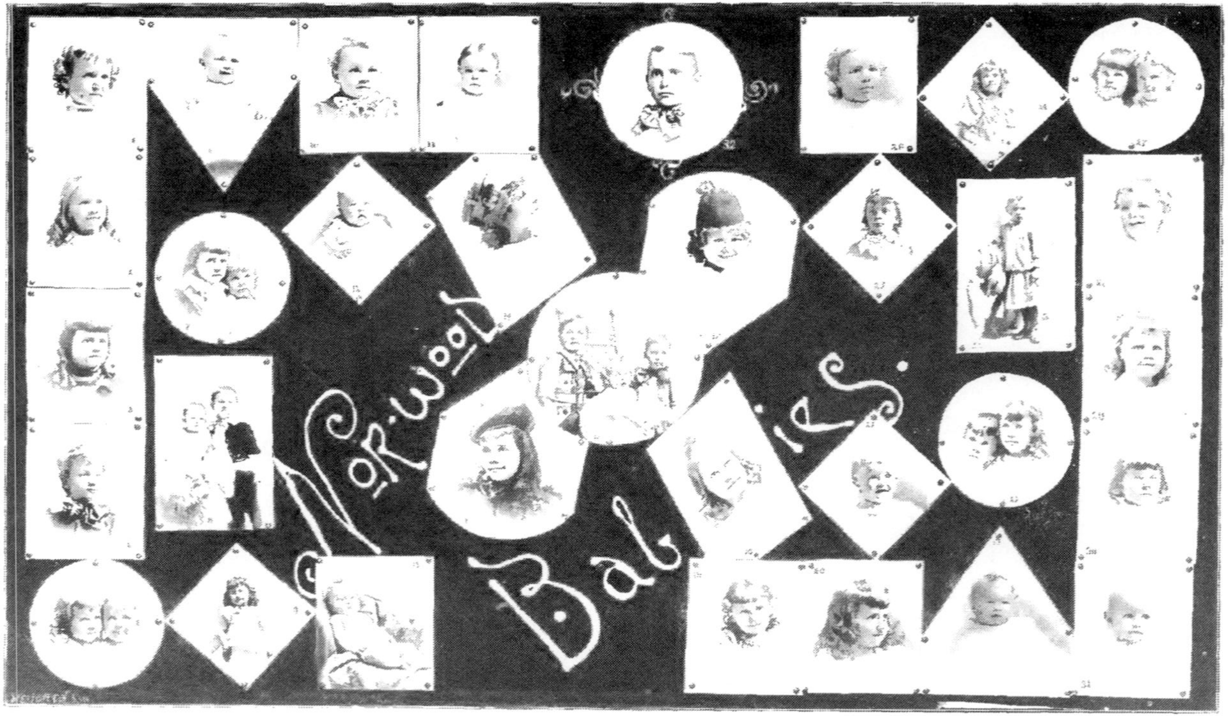

MAKING THE NORWOOD PRESSED BRICK.

PLENTEOUS in attractions, there is no more interesting place in the village than the brick works. That is Norwood's one great industry and it has added to the ever-increasing fame of the suburb. Located on the tract just above Duck Creek, and at the junction of the B. & O. S. W. railroad, there could be no improvement in situation, and a spur from the main track affords easy facilities for loading the output into the cars for transportation by rail. "The Norwood Brick" is famous, and the process of its manufacture a pleasing study. The plant of the Cincinnati Pressed Brick Company embraces seventy-five acres of ground. As 650,000 bricks are figured to the acre, a foot deep, and excavations are made ten times that deep, there is clay enough there to last a hundred years or so. In its crude state the earth is of a yellowish hue, but the bricks come from the burning in exquisite tints of red ranging from dark to light pink. The clay shed is the first stopping point made in the art of manufacture. After the clay has been dried by ploughing and harrowing, it is carted into that spacious building to undergo a sweating process, as it lies piled up under cover waiting for the second operation. Over in one corner of this shed a pair of ponderous rollers, weighing two tons apiece, revolve in a great pan, and though it is perforated beneath, the clay, which has been dumped therein, sifts. The finer particles are carried automatically to a height of forty feet by elevator cups, and emptied into the screen, which covers the hopper that feeds the brick-making machine, while the coarser are returned to the dry pan to be ground once more under the heavy rollers. Not a drop of water is used, and from the dry powder there are pressed bricks, each one of which weighs seven and one-half pounds. Each brick undergoes a pressure of 150,000 pounds. The capacity of the machinery is 80,000 a day, and to see the green bricks as they are really turned out, all it requires is to help oneself to chemistry. They are taken direct on trucks, the doors of which are not wood, of iron, and then piled up in such a manner that the fire may have full play through them, when it is torch is ready to be applied. There are five kilns at the plant, each with a capacity

of 200,000. With the kiln filled, comes the most important part of the work. Dry as those green bricks appear to be, there is nearly one-half pound of natural moisture in each one, and when the kiln is sealed nearly fifty tons of water must be dried out before they are ready for the burning. This process is called "water smoking," and is a gradual one. Low wood fires are kept burning from eight to eleven days, for an intense heat at that stage would crack and ruin the product. With the water smoking ended, then comes the firing, with oil. Crude petroleum is used and vaporized by jets of steam, a revolving current of flame roars through the kiln, without cessation, for eight or nine days. Hot is a mild sort of word to use. Old Belzebub himself would need a fan within that fiery furnace. In the burning, there is an eight or nine inch contraction, and from the settle the watchers know when it is time to put out the fires. The cooling off is as gradual as the drying out; but when the kiln is ready to be emptied, the setting of the bricks is the biggest single item in the whole cost of manufacture. No less than fifteen shades are revealed—so rich and warm that it seems almost impossible to believe that the tints are nature's own.

In addition to the "native output," a buff brick is also manufactured. It is made from a blue Indiana clay, the refuse from coal mines. Another novelty, a pink buff, is made from a central Ohio fire clay. In reds, buffs, browns and mottled, all shades of pressed brick can be had, and besides these about five million common bricks are made every year. When all the branches are in operation, sixty men are employed, and it is a remarkable fact that since the plant was opened (not quite three years ago), nearly all the output has been used in Cincinnati and vicinity. "The Norwood brick" has found a home market and has not been obliged to seek outside channels of trade. The Cincinnati Pressed Brick Company is officered as follows: W. A. Barker, President; L. D. Barker, Vice-President, and J. H. Barker, Secretary and Treasurer. The first two named are residents of Norwood, and their handsome home, on Park avenue, can be put in evidence to prove the possibilities of architectural beauty when their pressed brick is used. The Norwood Pumping station, the Cincinnati Club House, on Walnut Hills, the Methodist Book Concern, Albert Chatfield's new home, on Madison pike, the Hotel Alms, the German Old Men's Home, in Avondale, and St. Philip's Church, on Race street, Cincinnati, are only a few of the buildings in which the Norwood brick predominates. The company's downtown office is at 50 West Fourth, in the Perin Building.

Look at the Dwellings Built by

BOFINGER & HOPKINS

For the following Persons in Norwood.

William W. Addams,	George Eulor,	W. F. Brown,	A. H. Pape,
Charles G. B. Aydelott,	Victoria Fricke,	E. P. Hopkins,	H. J. Pfister,
Frederick Arnsmaier,	Herman Ferdleman,	Franc L. Hipel	Chas. B. Patton,
E. G. Bolles,	Fred. C. Fisher	Fred E. Hulidl	Edward Pape,
William Becker,	William Ferris,	O. F. Jones,	E. Riddel,
W. E. Bassett,	Gus A. Flatton,	Jos. Jones,	C. W. Ross,
G. M. Beckner,	John Fusner,	R. W. Jewell,	Theo. C. Ruzicka,
Charles T. Bousman,	William Geiger,	A. B. Kruse,	Clinton C. Robinson,
Helen J. Bowler,	G. W. Gale,	S. S. Kingery	S. F. Ross,
A. E. Bagge	Parker Gale,	Charles Kerner,	Henry Rheude,
William Brandhorst	J. K. Graybill,	L. B. Karr,	Fried. Ross,
A. M. Berens,	L. B. Green,	H. W. Kent,	C. A. Reinhart,
Ann F. Barton,	F. J. Grossheim,	Alfred Kopf,	H. J. Reedy,
E. M. Brown,	Charles F. Gage,	Ed. Klok,	W. W. Riley,
O. E. Bell,	A. C. Gale,	E. A. King,	Fred Kirner
J. H. Boos,	Lydia P. Graves,	Gilles Koerlar,	D. J. Stump,
Charles Brinkmeyer,	C. P. Hesser,	Peter Keller,	H. C. Suskes,
Henry Beggs,	C. M. Hattersley,	W. B. Kinkead,	F. H. Steinkamp
J. M. Baker,	John B. Hart, Forest ave	J. A. Knupp,	Mary Stagge
Ralph P. Bellsmith,	John B. Hart,	E. L. Kirk,	M. A. Sleen
W. G. Brown	John B. Hart,	Robt. Leslie	A. H. Singer,
A. A. Bassett,	John B. Hart	E. E. Lloyd	John Schenk,
W. E. Buckton,	John B. Hart, Lorai ave,	G. W. Lamb,	J. W. Singer
Robert Brock,	John B. Hart,	W. R. McGinnty	M. A. Sackett,
Herbert Bristow	John B. Hart,	Ken Midford, Jr	J. M. Thomson
W. F. Bonner,	John B. Hart,	C. G. Moulinier,	M. Teyert,
A. C. Cattell,	A. F. Hollis,	J. S. Miller,	H. J. Tuttle,
Samuel S. Cooper,	J. M. Harper,	Alex. Meller	Theo. Trinble
Sidney J. Charlesworth,	E. W. Holt,	Philip Muessinger	R. F. Taylor
Harrison A. Crosby,	J. E. Hofstatter,	David K. Mason,	J. S. Thompson,
W. J. Carey	Herbert L. Harrington,	Henry Merkle,	R. W. Wickersham
E. P. Crotty	Aug. Hinderstain,	John Moorwoson,	W. E. Widger,
S. A. Corkhill,	A. Hartman,	J. B. Meas,	Andrew Wenard,
Orris P. Cobb,	Jonathan Hattersley,	L. W. McGarvey,	E. F. Whitaker,
Harry Coates,	A. P. Hagenayer,	K. A. McAlister	H. C. Williams,
Charles W. Evans,	Harry C. Hey	S. E. Morgan,	Daniel Whitehead,
B. P. Edwards,	M. E. Hordy,	Loan Morgan,	C. A. Wilson,
G. P. Evans	Charles F. Hughes	S. B. Mulliand,	Caroline Weinland
Richard Evans,	F. C. Hock,	Fred J. Myers,	M. M. Williamson,
H. M. Edmondson,	John Howie,	W. B. Norton,	Geo. Webb,
W. H. Everhart,	James Humble	Thomas Newbigger,	Chas. Wrentz
Conner P. Davis,	Richard Hemple,	J. E. Sneke,	Ada Wahl,
Leopold Dressel,	Geo. T. Hipple	Francis S. Neal,	John Meyer,
Matthew DeBrunn,	C. G. Hallam	John Ochs,	W. F. Zoller,
Margaret P. Bertoh,	P. G. Hill,	Otto Otten	J. P. Zimmermann

Houses marked with (*) star, see picture in this book

THE above property represents a total value of $1,173,029.25. We are the proprietors of the 1st and 2d & 3d divisions of South Norwood, Bofinger & Hopkins Subdivision of East Norwood, and Bofinger & Hopkins 1st and 2d Subdivisions of the Drake Tract, Norwood. We will build for purchasers of lots, on small cash payment. Prospective purchasers can have the benefit of the 350 different plans of modern dwellings, in file at our office, or we prepare plans and specifications, after their own ideas, for purchasers of lots, without cost.

BOFINGER & HOPKINS,
236 Main Street.

Telephone 1475. CINCINNATI, OHIO.

Des Jardins & Hayward,

Rooms 75 and 76
Blymyer Building,
216 Main Street,
CINCINNATI.

ARCHITECTS

ARCHITECTS OF THE FOLLOWING BUILDINGS IN NORWOOD:
Presbyterian Church, C. L. and N. Depot, Residences of Jackson Slane, C. E. Page, C. L. Seaman, E. Mills, C. C. Robinson, A. A. King, J. R. Lindsay and L. M. Brown.

Guns, Rifles, Revolvers

AMMUNITION

AND GENERAL
Sporting
Goods

The Bandle Arms Co.

256 Main St.

FISHING TACKLE,

Base Ball and Athletic Goods

G. C. Riordan & Co.

Churches,
Public and Private
Buildings,
and Figure
Windows, Etc.

Artistic
Stained Glass
Workers,

30 and 32 East Fifth St.,
Cincinnati.

Designs and Estimates Furnished.

First Last and All the Time!

Fechheimer's

Men's **CLOTHING** Boys'

Quality the Best.
Prices the Lowest

HUNSTMAN & HARDESTY.

Florists and
Cut Flower Dealers

37 and 39 W. Fourth St., CINCINNATI.
Telephone 947.

HENRY LASANCE,

RESIDENCE:
IVANHOE AVENUE,
NORWOOD.

TAILOR.

No. 159 Main Street,
CINCINNATI.

The "Cincinnati Columbian Seal" Spoon.

THE SPOON FOR THE COLUMBIAN YEAR.

THE DUHME COMPANY, GOLDSMITHS AND SILVERSMITHS,
FOURTH AND WALNUT STREETS.

Choice Norwood Residences and Lots

For Sale by **GEO. F. DAVIS, Jr.,**

Real Estate and Loan Broker.

RESIDENCE:
Williams Avenue, West of
Ivanhoe Avenue,
NORWOOD.

OFFICE:
No. 52 Johnston Building,
5th and Walnut, at noon.
CINCINNATI.

To the Gentlemen, Gentle-women, and we trust, Gentle Children, of Norwood——

Browning, King & Co.
Race and 5th sts.
Cincinnati.

Rightly made Men's and Boys' Clothing at right prices; That's all——

Kelley Coal Coke

BUY THE BEST POCAHONTAS

FOR

Furnace, Stove and Grate.

Get my prices and terms before laying in your Winter supply. Anthracite and Bituminous Coal at lowest prices.

C. H. KELLEY,

MAPLE AVENUE,   NORWOOD, OHIO.

The Gem City Roofing and Paving Co.

OF DAYTON OHIO.

HAVE added greatly to the beauty of our Village by the laying of substantial Cement Walks. They have laid

Over Twelve Miles of Cement Walks

in Hamilton County in the past five years, and villages contemplating doing this kind of work, would do well by communicating with the above Company.

15 N. ST. CLAIR STREET,
DAYTON, O.

J. P. Zimmerman and Sons,

Telephone 488.   Nos. 126 and 128 Sycamore Street.

J. P. ZIMMERMAN,
J. P. ZIMMERMAN, JR.
E. J. ZIMMERMAN.

MANUFACTURERS OF
Hair and Spring Mattresses.

RESTORERS OF
Antique and Fine Furniture of Every Description.——

Upholsterers,

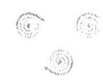

Attend to every Detail of Packing and Shipping and Storing Household Effects

DURRELL'S SUBDIVISION

On the **IVANHOE** Grand Boulevard.

SPECIAL ADVANTAGES.

High Location.   Private Sale only.
Dry Cellars.   Investment Protected.
Acceptable Parties and   Nearness to City and
Good Improvements only.   Every Convenience.

For proof of what we say examine the Property.

NO ADVANCE IN PRICES AT PRESENT.
LEASES AT LONG TIME, LOW RATES WILL BE GIVEN.

Call on DURRELL BROS., Esplanade Building.

The Union Central Life Insurance Co.

of Cincinnati

ASSETS OVER $11,000,000.

Our **Life-Rate Endowments**
  Are Profitable

Our **Twenty-Payment Guaranties**
  Are Economical.

Our **20-Payment Income Installments**
  Are Convenient and Inexpensive.

J. M. PATTISON, Pres.   E. P. MARSHALL, Sec'y.
E. W. JEWELL, General Agent.

BEHR BROS.
EMERSON   **PIANOS**
WURLITZER

Guitars, Mandolins, Autoharps, Violins,
And Everything in the Musical Line.

Call and Hear the **REGINA,** The New Music Box.
Plays any Number of Tunes.

THE RUDOLPH WURLITZER CO.

23 West Fourth Street.

GO TO

The Mabley & Carew Co.

OPPOSITE FOUNTAIN, CINCINNATI,

FOR

MEN'S AND BOYS' CLOTHING, Hats, Shoes, Furnishing Goods.

LADIES', MISSES' AND CHILDREN'S

Cloaks, Shoes, Millinery,

Underwear, Corsets and Gloves.

CHINA AND QUEENSWARE.

Gentlemen's Ladies' and Juvenile **WHEELS**

At Prices Where all can Afford to Ride.

Who says so?

RIDERS,

BESIDES THE MANUFACTURERS BACK THEM UP. WHAT WHEELS ARE THEY TALKING ABOUT?

THE FALCONS!

They are made at Yost Station.

We do not charge you for our catalogue. Send for one and learn how good wheels are made.

THE YOST MANUF'G CO.
TOLEDO, OHIO.

LOWEST RATES TO ALL PARTS OF THE WORLD.

RAILROAD TICKETS
BOUGHT AND SOLD.

Schiely & Poage,

TICKET BROKERS,

Members American Ticket Brokers Association.

193 Vine St. CAREW BUILDING. **107** Central Ave. NEAR GRAND CENTRAL DEPOT.

CINCINNATI.

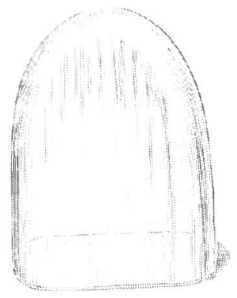

GLASS SHADES for covering and protecting fine ornamental Goods, Clocks, Bronzes, Statues, Etc.

Dinner, Tea and Toilet Sets,

Goods Delivered Free of Charge.

In all the latest Shapes and Decorations. Rich Cut Glass, Japanese China, A. D. Coffees, Lamps, Table Cutlery, Hotel and House Furnishing Goods, and China and Glassware of Every Description.

C. E. BROCKMANN, WHOLESALE AND RETAIL DEALER.

Nos. 110 and 112 MAIN STREET, East Side, bet. 3d and 4th Sts.   CINCINNATI, OHIO.

C. & A. KREIMER CO.

Nos. 373 to 381 MAIN STREET,
Factories, Richmond and Carr Streets.

FURNITURE!

Largest Assortment, Latest Designs, Select Styles, Lowest Prices.

Norwood

"The brightest diadem in the Queen City's beautiful coronet of suburbs."

POTTER'S

114 and 116 W. Fifth Street,   CINCINNATI

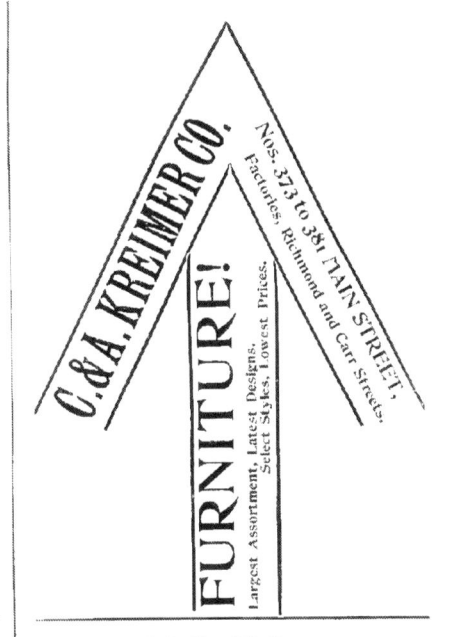

PIANOS!

Baby Grands and Uprights

- Decker Bros.,
- Baldwin,
- Fischer,
- Haines Bros.,
- Estey Piano Co.,
- Ellington,
- and other Pianos.

CASH or Payments.
OLD PIANOS taken in exchange.
PIANOS Tuned and Repaired.

D. H. BALDWIN & CO.

158 West Fourth Street,
NEAR ELM STREET.   CINCINNATI.

The PAPER

Used in this Publication was furnished by

The Chatfield & Woods Co.
237 and 239 W. Fourth St.
CINCINNATI, O.

THE A. E. Burkhardt Company.

Remodeling, Storage and Renovating of Furs.

WE beg leave to call your attention to the advantage of having Repairs and Alterations of Furs made during the Summer months, more careful workmanship is possible, and there is a considerable saving in cost.

We send for Fur and Winter Wraps, and insure at a moderate expense against loss from Fire, Moth or Burglary. The beneficial effect on Furs of our treatment during the Summer is alone worth the entire cost of storage.

THE A. E. Burkhardt Company
Furriers
258 and 260 Race Street.

The H. and S. Pogue Company
108 to 116 West 4th Street.

THE POPULAR and reliable "HEADQUARTERS" for all kinds of FOREIGN and DOMESTIC Dry Goods in SELECT ASSORTMENT and at MODERATE prices; always catering to every TASTE and PURSE, and carefully watching the Interest of our Customers.

The H. and S. POGUE CO.
108 to 116 West Fourth Street.
NORWOOD DELIVERY
Wednesday and Saturday.

The Northwestern Mutual Life Insurance Co.
of Milwaukee, Wis.

Incorporated in 1858.
Purely Mutual.

Assets, January 1, 1894,	$64,081,182.98
Liabilities, " " (4% reserve)	52,712,726.18
Surplus " "	11,358,456.80

I INVITE special attention to the character of the Northwestern, believing that no policy of life insurance issued by any other company approaches it as a desirable investment. No less dollar for dollar as an insurance contract...

M. J. MACK, GENERAL AGENT.
United Bank Building, Third and Walnut Streets,
CINCINNATI, O.

The Addyston Pipe and Steel Co.

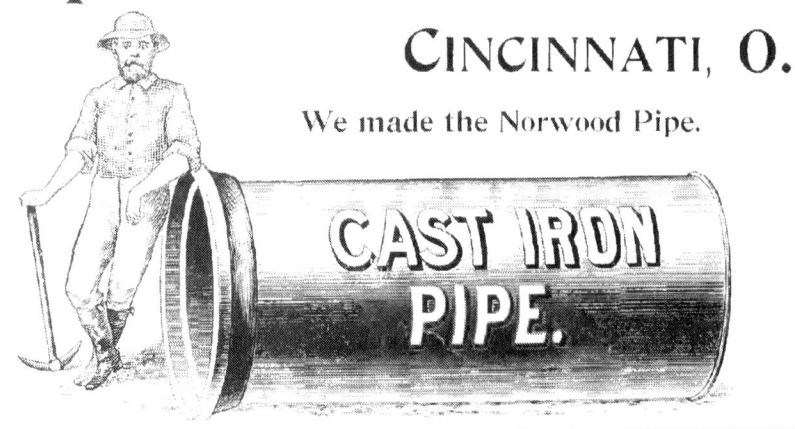

CINCINNATI, O.

We made the Norwood Pipe.

CAST IRON PIPE.

C&O ROUTE

TRANSACT BUSINESS in Cincinnati one day and in New York the next, only by taking the F.F.V. LIMITED, 12:20 noon, arriving at Washington 7:40 A.M., New York 1:40 P.M. The only Electric Lighted Train with Observation cars and the only train serving every meal en route in DINING cars.

F.F.V. FAST FLYING VIRGINIAN

OUR PUBLICATIONS

McCULLOUGH'S
SEED CATALOGUE
AND
···· AMATEUR'S GUIDE ····
Issued in January

McCullough's Catalogue of Fall Bulbs,
AND HOW TO GROW THEM
Issued in September

ESTABLISHED 1838

J. M. McCULLOUGH'S SONS
Seedsmen and Importers of Bulbs
134-136 WALNUT STREET

CINCINNATI, O.

ALBERT McCULLOUGH

TELEPHONE 584

TRADE MARK

TRAXEL & MAAS,

Art · Store
AND
Fine Art Gallery, 172 West Fourth St.

Artists' Supplies, Fine Pictures & Frames.

If you have any framing to do, give us a trial. We do the neatest and cleanest work in the city, at reasonable prices.

TELEPHONE 1610.

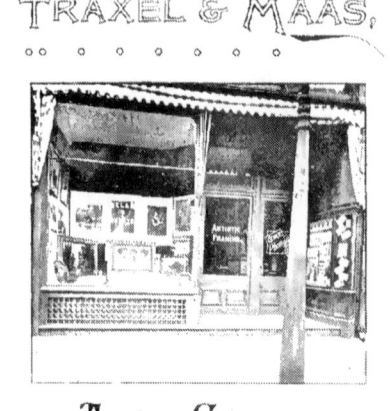

Hohnstedt & Windhorst

N. W. Cor. Main and Twelfth Streets.

Dry Goods and Notions

Lace Curtains	Dress Goods	Ladies' and Gents'
AND	A	Furnishing
Portieres.	Specialty.	Goods.

NORWOOD Delivery Daily.

For Norwood Real Estate

CALL ON

Moessinger, Fritsch & Hugle

AUCTIONEERS,
REAL ESTATE AND LOAN BROKERS.

No. 1 West Fourth Street.　　　　　　　　Cincinnati.

Norwood Park·····

Lies in the Very Center of the "Gem of the Highlands,"

And Contains 103 BEAUTIFUL BUILDING LOTS, Size, 50x150 Feet.

RESIDENCE OF A. Y. REID

It is within ONE SQUARE from Norwood ELECTRIC RAILWAY
One Square from B. & O. S. W. Depot, in East Norwood,

And is approached directly upon leaving the cars of the C., L. & N. R. R., at the station, which bears the name of "Norwood Park." The main thoroughfare, Park Avenue, is 110 feet wide, with a Park of 34 feet in the center, and an asphalt roadway on each side (see engraving page 51).

Floral Avenue is of the same width, with the roadway on each side paved with brick, sewers and artificial stone cement walks have been laid throughout the entire length of these Avenues.

All lots are uniformly graded and lie 2 feet above the curb grade and have perfect drainage.

We have none of the burdens of down-town smoke, soot, miasma and noise, but charming views for even the most enthusiastic lovers of Nature.

The location of "NORWOOD PARK" is unexcelled and is fast increasing in value. Handsome residences have just been built right on and adjoining the property. Montgomery Road will be converted into an 80-foot boulevard, paved with asphalt or brick, without cost to the purchasers of lots. The neighborhood is already established and is of a high character. Churches, Schools, Post-office, Telegraph and Telephone Stations and stores within convenient distance.

Perfect title guaranteed. Plats of the property, with prices, will be cheerfully furnished upon application.

A. Y. REID, Trustee.   Residence:
Office, 101 & 103 East 8th St., CINCINNATI, O.   CORNER PARK AND FLORAL AVENUES.

Telephone No. 101.

NORWOOD DIRECTORY.

JOHN L. VINE,
....Prescription Druggist,
STATIONS.
Post-Office.
Telephone.
Telegraph.

Montgomery Avenue, Opp. Central School Building,

NORWOOD, OHIO.

OPEN DAY & NIGHT.

FRANK GERDE,
Practical · Horse · Shoer,
MAIN AVE., NORWOOD, OHIO.

Special Attention Given to DRIVING HORSES.

HERMAN SCHUERMAN,
House Painting and Calcimining.

Montgomery Pike, North of Highland Ave. Norwood.

FRANK GRABUTH,
TIN AND SLATE ROOFING AND GALVANIZED CORNICE WORK.
DEALER IN Hardware and Tinware, STOVE CASTING.
Jobbing Promptly Attended To.
NORWOOD, OHIO.

F. SHAFER & CO.
Livery and Boarding Stable
MAIN AVENUE,
End of Electric Road. - - NORWOOD, O.

F. GRIEME,
N. W. Cor. Carter and Hopkins Aves
NORWOOD, O.

Druggist and Apothecary.

ICE COLD SODA WATER drawn from Matthews Apparatus with Syrups in GLASS JARS.

Prescriptions carefully and accurately compounded at all hours.

H. P. SMITH & SON,
.... MAIN AVENUE, OPPOSITE SCHOOL HOUSE.

The Norwood Home Store, Dry Goods & Notions,
AT CITY PRICES.

Leading GROCERY Of the Village,
JOHN NIEHAUS,
DEALER IN
Staple and Fancy Groceries.
MAIN ROAD, NORWOOD, OHIO.

The Pioneer Barber Shop of Norwood
PHIL. VOELKER, Prop'r.

Montgomery Road, near the B. & O. S. W. Bridge.

COMPETENT ASSISTANTS IN ATTENDANCE.

WM. SCHUELER,
DEALER IN BOOTS, SHOES AND RUBBERS,
Custom Work, Repairing Neatly Done.

Montgomery Boulevard. - Opposite School House.

SMOKE
"LA DUCHESSE"
5c * CIGARS. * 5c.
JOHN L. VINE, Agent.
NORWOOD. OHIO.

The above Cut Represents a Handsome and Artistic Residence on the Northeast Corner of Hudson and Floral Avenues.

What is Elsmere?

OUR present Prices range from $10 to $50 per ft., according to location and street.

ELSMERE Consists of [illegible] acres of the finest residence property in Hamilton County, being within easy distance of Fountain Square. The ground is in the form of a plateau, and therefore has the best natural drainage.

ELSMERE Is beautifully situated, being located east of the Montgomery pike, and forms the most southern portion of the village of Norwood, bounded on the north by Williams avenue; on the east by the Duck Creek road; on the south by Lexington avenue, and on the west by Regent avenue.

ELSMERE Improvements consist of made streets, sidewalks, sewers, tree-planting and forty beautiful homes, all of which have been built very recently.

FLORAL Avenue, the principal street, is [illegible] feet wide, paved, with [illegible]

Transportation facilities are good. The Mt. Adams and Eden Park electric [illegible] Fountain Square [illegible] Lexington [illegible] Hudson or Williams [illegible] C. P. & V. R. R. [illegible] Elsmere [illegible] property.

ELSMERE Has good shipping facilities. Cars from any point [illegible] on the Elsmere siding, thereby facilitating building operations, as coal, lumber, stone, brick, sand and all other kinds of material can be delivered at a lower rate than by a long haul with teams.

ELSMERE Is surrounded with fine improvements on all sides. A visit to Elsmere will convince any one that we have, without a doubt, the finest property for the price in the vicinity of Cincinnati, and never was there an opportunity given to Cincinnati people of securing a home on terms more favorable.

The projected improvement of Montgomery pike alone will add [illegible] to the present value of Elsmere property.

OFFICE: Elsmere R. R. Station C. P. & V. R. R.
and Room 23 Johnston Building, CINCINNATI.

JOHN G. BROTHERTON & CO.

Water Works

Means a number of comforts for us, and while a good

Bath

Can be counted as a necessary rule of the Health Officer, not saying anything of the comforts gained thereby; your lawns need a certain amount of attention, and

Seamless Tube Rubber Hose

can not be dispensed with. We are the only

Manufacturers

In Cincinnati, and assure you not only goods second to none, but prices to suit every purse. We own and control the patents for making Hose, with a

Seamless Tube.

Cleveland Rubber Works,
248 Race Street,
CINCINNATI.

W. G. Brown,
MANAGER.

G. W. Rucker, President. ... Donnelly, Vice President
Geo. A. Loeb, Sec'y and Treas.

The Rucker Stone Company.

OFFICE AT
GREENFIELD, OHIO.

GRAVEL BANK,
West Loveland.

Cleaned Screened Gravel for Streets, Pikes, Concrete Sidewalks, Etc.

STONE QUARRIES,
Greenfield & Hillsboro,
OHIO.

Screened Crushed Lime Stone, Curb, Crosswalk, Flagging, Building and Dimension Stone, Lime, Etc.

Baltimore and Ohio Southwestern R'y.

THE HISTORY of Norwood would be incomplete without mention of the advantages which have been offered to its builders and residents by the Baltimore and Ohio Southwestern Railway. The first road to be constructed, it early saw the advantages to be derived from a suburban service to Norwood, and that it has successfully met the demands for this service is evinced by the number of trains which are run each week day to and from Cincinnati. It also offers to new residents a free ticket for one year for any one building a house costing not less than $1,000. It offers many other good things. Ask for a copy of "Suburban Homes" and "Suburban Trains" at Ticket Office, S. E. Corner Fourth and Vine Streets, Cincinnati, or of the Agent at Norwood.

Our Cars.

PROFESSIONAL CARDS.

DAVID DAVIS
Rooms 60 & 61, Johnston Buildings
Attorney at Law,
CINCINNATI, O.
Telephone ---

CHARLES E. PRIOR,
Attorney at Law,
Room 45, Carew Building,
N. W. Corner Fifth and Vine Streets.
CINCINNATI.
Telephone No. 189.

COBB & HOWARD,
Telephone 316
ATTORNEYS AND COUNSELORS AT LAW
Blymyer Building, 216 Main St., CINCINNATI.
ORRIS P. COBB, Residence, Norwood.
EDWIN J. HOWARD, Residence, Price Hill.

WM. E. BUNDY
Attorney at Law and Notary Public,
RESIDENCE, N.W. Cor Ivanhoe and Wayland Avenues, NORWOOD.
ROOMS 210, 211, 212 LINCOLN INN COURT,
No. 227 MAIN STREET, CINCINNATI.
TELEPHONE 2100.

WILLIAM G. WILLIAMS
Attorney at Law,
No. 5 West Fourth Street,
Opp. the Highest steeple,
RESIDENCE, Carthage Ave., Norwood Heights.
CINCINNATI, O.

EDWARD MOULINIER,
Telephone 2000.
ATTORNEY AT LAW.
NOTARY PUBLIC.
Room 34 Blymyer Building, 216 Main Street,
RESIDENCE: Monroe Ave., bet. Forest and Floral Aves., Norwood.
CINCINNATI.

AARON McNEILL,
COUNSELOR AND ATTORNEY AT LAW,
SMITH BUILDING,
CINCINNATI, OHIO.

DR. R. C. WINTERMUTE,
MENTOR AVENUE,
THIRD DOOR WEST OF PIKE.
HOURS: 7 TO 10 A.M., 4 TO 7 P.M. AND EVENINGS
CITY OFFICE, 155 W. Seventh St.
HOURS 10:30 TO 2:30
TELEPHONE 1407.

JAMES A. GIBSON, No. 24 New Street, CINCINNATI, O.

BRANCH SHOP, Montgomery Road and Sherman Av., Norwood

Plumber, Gas and Steam Fitter.

NORWOOD. First Branch tapped ready for Water for Dr. Springer, May 22, 1894, at 12 o'clock Noon. Made by JAMES A. GIBSON.

JAMES A. GIBSON,

The Plumber of the Magnificent "Ortiz" Block, in October 29, 1882.

F. G. LEIMANN, Manufacturer and Builder

Ivanhoe, Hamilton Co., O.

☞ Before you build, it will be to your interest to get an estimate from me.

Sash, Doors, Blinds and General Mill Work.

WM. LAWSON & BRO.

SANITARY PLUMBERS

TELEPHONE 1453.

N. E. Cor. Eighth and Walnut Streets,

CINCINNATI.

The R. & R. Syrup
For Coughs and Colds.

OF WHITE PINE AND TAR.

PRICE, 25c. and 50c.

Manufactured by the **Roosa & Ratliff Chemical Co.**
CINCINNATI.

The Thomson & Blackman Company
Stationers, Engravers & Printers.

Makers of Crepe and Tissue Paper Art Novelties.

Retail Department, HARMS' PALAIS ROYAL, 64 and 66 W. Fourth St. } Cincinnati. { Manufacturing and Engraving Department, 64 W. Fourth Street.

Empsons
E. H. VAN ZANT, Prop'r.

Fine Confections.

Ladies' and Gentlemen's Dining Parlors.

72 W. Fourth Street, CINCINNATI.

GEO. F. OTTE, President.   F. L. RATTERMANN, Vice Pres.
C. E. SPIELMAN, Sec'y and Treas.   JNO. D. SAYERS, Gen Supt.

THE GEO. F. OTTE Company

CARPETS

CURTAINS AND DRAPERIES,

131 and 133 West Fourth Street,

CINCINNATI, O.

FINE GOLD JEWELRY,
RELIABLE WATCHES,
HIGH GRADE PRECIOUS STONES,
STERLING SILVERWARE,
BRIC-A-BRAC,
FINE ART GOODS,
BRONZE STATUARY,
MARBLE STATUARY,

BANQUET LAMPS
IN CHINA AND BRONZE,
CLOCKS AND ORNAMENTS,
ONYX PEDESTALS,
COALPORT,
CROWN DERBY,
VIENNA AND DRESDEN
WARES OF ART.

Importer and Manufacturer of **ENGLISH HALL CLOCKS.**

FRANK HERSCHEDE, Importing Jeweler,
179 Vine Street, Corner Arcade.

Queen City Supply Company.

161, 163, 165 W. Pearl St.
COR. ELM,
CINCINNATI.

PUCHTA, PUND & CO., Proprietors.

SUPPLIES OF EVERY DESCRIPTION FOR

Mills,
Factories,
Engineers,
Machine
    Shops.

Mines,
Railroads,
Lumbermen,
Contractors.

AGENTS FOR

Jewell Belting Co., Leather Belting.
Boston Belting Co., Rubber Goods.
Jno. A. Roebling's Sons Co., Wire Rope.
B. F. Sturtevant Co. Blowers, Fans and Exhausts.
Grant Corundum Wheel Co., Emery Wheels.
Standard Flint Paper Co., Sand and Emery Paper and Cloth.
Magnolia Anti-Friction Metal Co., and many others.

Cleneay & Van Antwerp,
No. 7 W. Fourth St. CINCINNATI.

OWNERS AND PROPRIETORS OF

CLENEAY SUBDIVISION NORWOOD **AND VAN ANTWERP SUBDIVISION** AVONDALE

.... Builders of Suburban Homes. ....
Our Terms are Easy.

Lots are the Choicest. Money to Loan on Real Estate
Plans and Specifications Furnished. at Lowest Rates.

The Portland Cement Pavement
Smooth, Dry and Durable.

IS THE Ideal Sidewalk of the Age.

In Laying Them we Use only the Best and HIGHEST PRICED CEMENT

THAT is imported. Our walks grow stronger with age, and have a fine, bluish-gray color that does not change. The elegance of our work, laid in Wyoming in 1889 and '90, caused cement to be laid in other villages. We use clean gravel and sand, but adulterates cement. We own a sand along Mill Creek, above Spring Grove, where we get washed sand and gravel.

We also lay these Sidewalks with
GRANITE SURFACE
CALLED
GRANITOID.

We lay Asphalt Floors, Roofs and Driveways.

The Chas. Kuhl Artificial Stone Co.
91, 93, 95 Canal, near Vine.

The College of Music
OF CINCINNATI.

An Eleemosynary Institution, Incorporated by the General Assembly of the State of Ohio.

**Amply Endowed.
Entire Income Devoted to Instruction.**

Furnishes a complete education in Vocal and Instrumental Music, Literature, Elocution and Oratory.
Large corps of able and experienced Professors.
Open throughout the year.
Summer Term June, July, August.
Students run every school day.
Normal Classes, Chorus Classes, Prima Vista Classes, Ensemble Classes, Orchestra Classes, Lectures, Rehearsals, Recitals, etc., are among the free privileges.

SPECIAL DEPARTMENT for Teachers of Music in the Public Schools.

PETER RUDOLPH NEFF, President

SEND FOR CATALOGUE.

F. J. NOLAN. J. A. ARMLEDER.

Nolan & Armleder,
Superior Plumbers
PHONE 1943

No. 65 E. 4th St., CINCINNATI, OHIO.

HOT WATER HEATING.
STEAM FITTING.
GAS FITTING.

H. N. Weisbrodt
S. E. Cor. Fifth and Walnut Sts.

Designing and Engraving on Wood.
Photo-Engraving, Half-tone Zinc-Etching and Electrotyping.

Cincinnati.

True Distinction

"A House"

Such a House,

The John Shillito Company

1830 — 1894

J. E. Poorman,
5 W. Fifth Street.
BICYCLES & SUPPLIES.

FOR Summer Cooking,
"New Process" Vapor Stoves
Are Unexcelled,
Absolutely Safe,
Lights Like Gas.

Dodd, Werner & Co.
72 and 74 W. FOURTH ST.,
Gas Fixtures, Lamps and Supplies.

Electric Fixtures,
A complete line of Medium and Fine Patterns constantly on hand.
Inspection Solicited.

For baking of all kinds * * * *
* * * *   Ask your Grocer
             FOR

Fleischmann Co.'s
Compressed
Yeast.

Fresh Daily.   * * * * * * *

* * * * * * *   Notice Yellow Label.

ROBERT LESLIE'S
Real Estate
......Office

Hopkins Ave.
Station,
NORWOOD, O.

OFFICE HOURS
8 to 10 A M
3 to 5 P. M.

Mr. LESLIE has lots and houses for sale in all parts of NORWOOD, NORTH EVANSTON, IDLEWILD AND PLEASANT RIDGE.

Houses for Rent,
　　Stores for Rent,
　　　　Loans Negotiated.

"BIG FOUR"
TO
ST. LOUIS
AND
CHICAGO.
BEST LINE.

M. E. INGALLS,　　　E. O. McCORMICK,　　　D. B. MARTIN,
President.　　Passenger Traffic Manager.　　Gen'l Pass. and Ticket Agent.

CINCINNATI.

J. F. McCRACKEN, President. ED. S. GRANT, Gen'l Manager. T. F. McCLURE, Sec'y and Treas.

The Union Paving Co.

(INCORPORATED.)

Vitrified Paving Block and Sewer Brick.
Capacity, 120 Millions.

The Union Paver.
The Riverside Paver.
The Grant Block.
The Mack Block.
The McManigal Block.
The Ironton Block.
The Scioto Block.

WORKS AT
New Cumberland, W. Va.
Middleport, Ohio.
Ironton, Ohio.
Portsmouth, Ohio.

OFFICE:
No. 51 Goodall Building,
Telephone 174.   CINCINNATI, OHIO.

Lowest Price Piano House in the City.
Cash or Payments.

Smith & Weisenborn

195 and 197 WEST SEVENTH STREET,

HIGH GRADE Upright, Grand & Square **PIANOS** A Specialty.

PRICES
$75,
$150,
$175,
$200,
$235,
and up.

Hardman, Cook, Jewett, Vose & Sons, Decker, Weber, and other Makes.

Orders for Tuning Received at Smith's Residence, Mills Ave. and Carter St., Norwood.

JNO. ANDERSON, Pres't.   W. W. RILEY, Sec'y and Treas.

For Fine Work Try

The Model Laundry Co.

No. 47 West Fifth Street,

Fountain Square.

Norwood Delivery, Monday, Thursday and Saturday.

TELEPHONE 2014.

"We are Pioneers in Norwood."

HOCK & HOPKINS,

Plumbers and Gasfitters.

.... Special Attention Given to Sanitary Ventilation.

Montgomery Pike, Cor. Sherman Ave.

Bicycles and Athletic Goods

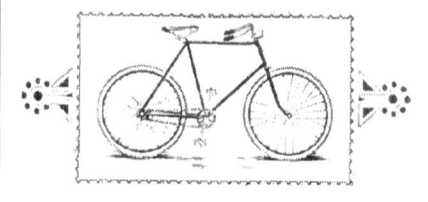

LARGEST STOCK
LOWEST PRICES

Chas. Hanauer & Bros.

DAVID FOLZ & SONS,

NOW Kirchner & Folz,

Richelieu Building,
S. E. Cor. 9th & Plum Sts.
CINCINNATI, O. .....

General Contractors

For the Construction of STREETS, SEWERS, ETC.

The Best Approved Appliances Used and

ALL WORK
GUARANTEED

As to Rapidity and Stability.

Some of the PRINCIPAL Avenues of Norwood were Built by this Firm.

DAVID FOLZ & SONS.

Your House is on Fire!

May be the warning you heard some night. You may simply have time to get your family out without stopping to secure those valuable papers, such as insurance policies, deeds, mortgages, notes, etc., that you have been keeping in a tin box. Why run such chances of having those valuable papers destroyed, and thus become involved in numerous law suits, when for

$20.00

we will sell you a

FINE FIRE-PROOF SAFE, which will stand the hottest of fires, and preserve its contents without their being marred or scorched. You will be surprised to see what an elegant SAFE we can sell you for the above amount. Call at our Factory and see for yourself.

The VICTOR SAFE AND LOCK CO.,
9th and Broadway, CINCINNATI, O.

Agents Wanted in every city and town in the United States. Over 300 Victor Safes have already passed through very severe fires, and not one has ever yet failed to preserve its contents.

Are You Married?

It is the small annoyances, like a lost collar-button, that fret and worry. Sour milk over night; no milkman in the morning; no cream for the coffee; no milk for the baby.

THE Gail Borden Eagle Brand

Condensed Milk is always ready for use. Use it for tea, coffee and chocolate; for ice cream, summer drinks, and general cooking purposes.

As an infant's food, IT HAS NO EQUAL.

This country is full of fat, healthy Babies raised on the Eagle Brand.

Liverpool and London and Globe INSURANCE CO.

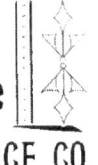

One of the foremost English Companies, Known the world over for its Unsurpassed Indemnity.

Cincinnati General Agency, 3d and Main,
J. M. DeCAMP, General Agent.

W. R. JOHNSON, Resident Agent in Norwood and Vicinity.
Also 95 Main Street.

Card Parties — Progressive Euchre, Etc.

In preparing for a card party, it is often difficult to obtain Playing Cards of equal quality, but different in design and rich coloring, for each table. The "Congress Playing Card Sets," made this season, embrace elegant "Congress," "Lenox" and "El Dorado" patterns, gold backs and gold edges, in greatest variety, making an assortment large enough for any lady giving a series of parties to select different patterns for each table and for each entertainment.

If your dealer does not keep the "Congress Sets," and will not get them, we will send you prepaid one or more sets of six packs each on receipt of $3.00 per set.

Duplicate Whist

"National" Method. Copyrighted also. Patent applied for.

With Whist Playing Cards, Index Cards, Score Cards, Rubber Bands and Illustrated Book of Rules, all ready for play, for $4.00. All explained in two lines:

Red sides of Index Cards govern original play.
Yellow sides of Index Cards govern duplicate play.

Costs less with Playing Cards than other methods without cards. For sale by dealers, or one sample six-pack set will be sent, expressage paid, on receipt of $4.00. Write for Illustrated Book of Rules.

The United States Printing Company,
Cincinnati, U. S. A.

PLAYING CARD MANUFACTORIES:
Russell & Morgan Factories.
National Factory.

"Card Games," authorized and illustrated, will be sent to any address for ten cents in stamps.

S.J. OSBORN, Jr., & Co.

Our Combined Curb and Gutter

Is far superior to and handsomer than anything ever used for the purpose. It is especially adapted to City Parks, Suburban Towns, Subdivisions, etc., etc. It is as strong as natural stone and guaranteed not to lose its alignment. It is endorsed by many of the leading engineers, and is used extensively in Cincinnati, Chicago and St. Louis.

Write for information.

S.J. Osborn, Jr., & Company,

CONTRACTORS FOR

Granitoid Combined Curb and Gutter

AND

Sidewalks,

Eggleston Av. & Pearl St.

CINCINNATI.

HIGHLAND ROUTE.
C., L. & N. Railway,

SUBURBAN TRAINS TO

IVANHOE, HOPKINS AVENUE, NORWOOD PARK, EAST NORWOOD, McCULLOUGH'S, LESTER, PLEASANT RIDGE, WOODFORD, KENNEDY, EUCLID, SILVERTON, DEER PARK, ROSSMOYNE, TERRE ALTA, BLUE ASH, MONTGOMERY.

LOW FARES. QUICK SERVICE.

THROUGH Trains to MASON and LEBANON, Stopping at the above Stations.

GEO. HAFER, President.   CLAY ROCKWELL, Gen'l Passenger Agent.

The Heart of Norwood.

ALL these advantages are found in the Subdivision made by Hedger and others, located West of the Montgomery Road, opposite the Main School Building.

Just the Place for Home Seekers.
Improved Streets, Cement Walks, Sewerage and Light.

THE TOWN HALL IS ON THIS **SUBDIVISION**

LOTS ALL FIFTY FEET FRONT. Located on Montgomery Road, Maple and Elm Avenues.

For Sale on Liberal Terms to Parties who will Make First-Class Improvements. Apply to

GEO. HAFER, CINCINNATI.

HAVE your Architect include a Billiard Room in his plans for your house. An apartment 13x17 feet will do. Billiards is the most delightful home amusement.

The Brunswick-Balke-Collender Co.
W. 6th Street, Cincinnati.

The largest residence in Norwood, commonly known as the "Capitol" of Norwood, belonging to Dr. A. Springer, was built from the designs of A. O. ELZNER, Architect, 227 Main Street, Cincinnati. Mr. Elzner also has built many other fine residences, besides public buildings such as the Neave Building, the Cincinnati Club, Yononte Inn, etc.

YALE
Paracentric Locks

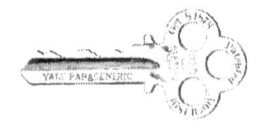

ACTUAL SIZE OF KEY.

GREATEST SECURITY.

THE YALE & TOWNE M'F'G COMPANY,

STAMFORD, CONN.

NEW YORK, CHICAGO, BOSTON, PHILADELPHIA, PITTSBURGH, SAN FRANCISCO.

W. J. BEHYMER & SON,
Norwood and Madisonville.

Wagons for Picnics and Light Hauling, Carriages furnished for Weddings and other Occasions.

Calls Answered Day and Night. **UNDERTAKERS**

LIVERY AND BOARDING STABLE.

TELEPHONES

W H STEWART, Jr.   G. S. STEWART.   H H STEWART

W. H. STEWART'S SONS,   Telephone 2161.

OFFICE AND MILL:
303, 305 and 307 Plum Street,
CINCINNATI.

Contractors.

J. WILDER & CO.

159 and 161 W. 6th St.
NEAR ELM.

General Agents **Philadelphia Lawn Mower,**
THE BEST MANUFACTURED.
ALSO DEALERS IN
Garden and Flower Seeds, Lawn Grass Seeds, Fertilizers, and Lawn Supplies, Fruit and Shade Trees, Shrubbery, Roses and Small Fruits. Poultry Supplies.

IMPORTERS OF
WINTER and SPRING FLOWERING BULBS.

J. FRIEDEBORN, MANAGER.

E. W. WHITE & Company

FINE BAKERY GOODS

AND LUNCHEON.

79 West Fourth Street,

NEAR VINE.

WHITE STAR LAUNDRY CO.

S. B. WATERS, Secy. & Treas. C. G. WATERS, Manager.

We call and deliver TWICE A WEEK IN NORWOOD.

The only Laundry in the United States that received a medal for Fine Laundry Work.

FOR those that appreciate HIGH CLASS Laundry Work, we do the work by HAND, which will SUIT THE MOST FASTIDIOUS, as it is done by the most skilled help obtainable in the country

202 RACE STREET.

TELEPHONE 460-2.

Within Your Reach.

HATS

All the most fashionable Styles of

Derby and Alpine **HATS**

IN ALL QUALITIES.

WM. L. THEIS & CO.

HATTERS,

161 Main Street, near Fourth, CINCINNATI, O.

Cincinnati Society of Decorative Art.

In charge of MISS CURRY, formerly of the WOMAN'S EXCHANGE.

142 & 144 West 7th Street, Between RACE AND ELM.

Embroidery Materials and Stamping. Royal and Mexican Drawn Work. Novelties in Woman's Work sold on commission.

Home-Made Cakes, Rolls, Croquettes, Etc.

LUNCH Served from 11 to 4 Daily.

We Solicit Your Patronage.

Koch & Braunstein.

CHINA AND GLASSWARE.

Artistic Pottery, Fine Table Cutlery.

68 & 70 W. 4th St., Opposite Pike's Opera House,

Formerly 112 West Fifth Street.

E. J. MALDEN.   WM. G. MALDEN.

Malden Bros.

PLUMBERS AND GAS FITTERS,

320 Main Street, CINCINNATI, O.

And MONTGOMERY ROAD, North of Hopkins Avenue Depot, NORWOOD, OHIO.

Bissinger's

FINE FRENCH CONFECTIONS.

169 VINE, NEAR FOURTH.   -   CINCINNATI, OHIO.

THE POUNSFORD STATIONERY CO.

Blank Book Manufacturers.
Fine Stationery & Engraving.
LAWN TENNIS.

LOWEST PRICES AND LARGEST STOCK.

3 West 4th, 149 Main St.,   -   CINCINNATI, OHIO.

FRED. MOLLENKAMP.   HENRY BINNE.

Mollenkamp & Binne,

Manufacturers of The Improved   CHAMPION **WASHING MACHINE,**

Patented Feb. 8, 1887.

No. 55 Canal St.

Bet. Walnut & Vine Sts.,

CINCINNATI, O.

WRINGERS Sold & Repaired.

F. MOLLENKAMP, Residence, Sherman Ave., NORWOOD, O.

Feldman's

NORWOOD HEIGHTS **SUBDIVISION.**

High Ground.
Lots: 50x160.

TERMS REASONABLE.

✸

Resides on Premises.

M. A. McGuire,

Trunk, Valise & Satchel Manufacturer.

No. 172 Walnut Street.   Repairing & Sample Work a Specialty.

Factory, No. 34 E. 5th St., CINCINNATI, O.

OLIVER SCHLEMMER.

Steam and Hot Water Heating Engineer.

PLUMBING AND GAS FITTING. 437 Linn Street, and 131 Charlotte Street.

Exclusive Agent for the **SPENCE** Hot Water Heater.

Ashley Lloyd's residence equipped with the SPENCE Heater.

Estimates Cheerfully Furnished.   Telephone 7580.

The Ault & Wiborg Co.
Makers of
Letter-Press and Lithographic
Printing Inks
Cincinnati, O.
U.S.A.
Branches: New York, Chicago.

HIC ET UBIQUE

The Ink used on this Publication is from the above house.

HESS & CO.
BUILDERS OF
Fine Carriages and Wagons.

Main and Highland Avenues, Norwood, Ohio.

REPAIRING NEATLY DONE.

JAMES M. HARPER,

Surveyor and Civil Engineer.

RICHELIEU BUILDING.

S. E. COR. NINTH AND PLUM STREETS.

Residence, Crown Avenue, - - NORWOOD.

CHAS. J. DAUNER,
WITH H. O. SCHELL & SON.

Fire, Marine, Accident, Steam Boiler, Life, Tornado and Plate Glass Insurance

No. 49 W. Third Street, Second Floor,

TELEPHONE 43.   CINCINNATI, O.

The Northern National Fire Insurance Co., of Milwaukee, Wis.

DEAR SIR:
Pursuant to instructions from the West Norwood Volunteer Fire Brigade, I am authorized to tender to you and your company a vote of thanks for the promptness with which you settled our claim for $685—the full amount of insurance carried on the house which was burned to the ground on March 4th, 1893. On March 14th, just ten days after the fire, a check was sent us for the full amount. This certainly bespeaks well for your method of doing business. Your promptness enabled us to rebuild at once a new engine house that we hope to make of much value as well as being of practical use to the village of Norwood. Wishing you and your company success, I am,

Very truly yours,

CHARLES H. WEISENFELDER, Sec'y.

WE ARE MANUFACTURERS OF FURNACES FOR HEATING & VENTILATING
CHURCHES, SCHOOLS, STORES, DWELLINGS. WRITE US FOR PRINTED MATTER.

JOHN GROSSIUS' SONS
389 MAIN ST. CINCINNATI, O.

RICHTER & WESSLING,

ARCHITECTS.....
AND SUPERINTENDENTS

Room 34 Johnston Building,
S. W. Cor. 5th and Walnut Streets,   CINCINNATI, O.

☞ Architects for the three School Buildings at Norwood. ☜

DRUCKER & CO.
MANUFACTURERS OF TRUNKS, VALISES, SATCHELS, TRAVELING EQUIPMENTS, LEATHER GOODS, ETC.

NO. 185 VINE ST. BELOW 5TH

JOHN W. HALL, CONTRACTOR

Builder of Brickwork for Norwood Pumping Station.

RESIDENCE, Ivanhoe Avenue.

Personal attention given to buildings erected by me. Special attention given to pressed-brick work.

The A. L. DUE Fire Works Co.

MANUFACTURERS OF THE CELEBRATED

Gold Medal Fine Colored High-Grade

Fire Works.

CINCINNATI, OHIO.

Contractors for Public Displays.

The grand display of FIRE WORKS at the dedication of the Norwood Water Works was made by the above-named Company.

Hiram S. Mathers
...REAL ESTATE BROKER.

Special Attention Given to Norwood Properties.

Real Estate Sold.
Loans Negotiated.
Dwellings, Flats, Stores and Factories Rented.
Real Estate and Chattels Auctioneered.
Estates and Subdivisions Managed.
Rents Collected.

68 and 70 West Fourth St.

Long Distance Telephone 1810.

The Dexter Lumber Co.

DEALERS AND MANUFACTURERS OF

White Pine, Poplar, Hemlock, Cypress, Cedar, and Yellow Pine.

Mill Work AND Lumber.

MOULDINGS, CASINGS, BASE, ETC.

IN ANY QUANTITIES, AT

VERY · LOW · PRICES.

NORWOOD, - - OHIO.

HENRY RANSHAW, Pres't. & Manager.   Wm. STACEY, Vice-Pres't.
THOS. H. BIRCH, Ass't Manager.   R. J. TARVIN, Sec'y & Treas.

The STACEY Manufacturing · Co.

GAS HOLDERS OF ALL STYLES AND SIZES.

IRON AND STEEL TANKS

For Gas Holders, Water or Oil.

PURIFIERS AND BENCH CASTINGS.

Office, No. 39 Mill Street. **CINCINNATI, O.**

Diploma and Medal of Highest Honor

AWARDED

The Everett Piano.

MADE BY THE EVERETT PIANO CO., BOSTON, MASS.

——BY——

The World's Columbian Exposition Jury of Awards.

AWARD.

For a full and sonorous tone.
For very good sustaining power.
For a smooth, well balanced scale.
For a superior action, well regulated, and of their own manufacture, possessing very good repeating qualities.
For an easy and elastic touch.

For the finest quality material used in construction.
For workmanship showing great care.
For well made cases.
The patent action brackets deserve special mention, saving time in removing and regulating the action.

Jury of Awards.

DR. F. ZIEGFELD, President Chicago Musical College.
V. J. HLAVAC, Musical Conductor, St. Petersburg, Rus.
GEO. STECK, Former Piano Manufr., New York City.
E F CARPENTER, Former Organ Mfr., Worcester, Mass.
MAX SCHIEDMAYER, Piano Manufr., Stuttgart, Ger.
DR. HUGH A. CLARKE, University of Pennsyla., Phila.

Signed:

GEO STECK, Judge.
K. BUENZ, President.
J. H. GORE, Secretary
and Chief Judge of Dept. of Liberal Arts.

The John Church Company,

GENERAL FACTORS.

CINCINNATI. NEW YORK. CHICAGO.

KNIGHT & CO.

THIS Souvenir is a Specimen of our Typographical Skill and Presswork.

Printers, Binders, Designers, Engravers.

CINCINNATI, OHIO.

Persons who contemplate issuing any sort of Publication, whether of a literary or advertising character, should not fail to confer with us before placing the order.

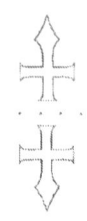

THE Laidlaw-Dunn-Gordon Company

OFFICES: 186 and 188 W. 2d St., CINCINNATI.
Factories: Cincinnati and Hamilton, O., U.S.A.

BUILDERS OF

STEAM PUMPING MACHINERY
FOR ANY SERVICE.

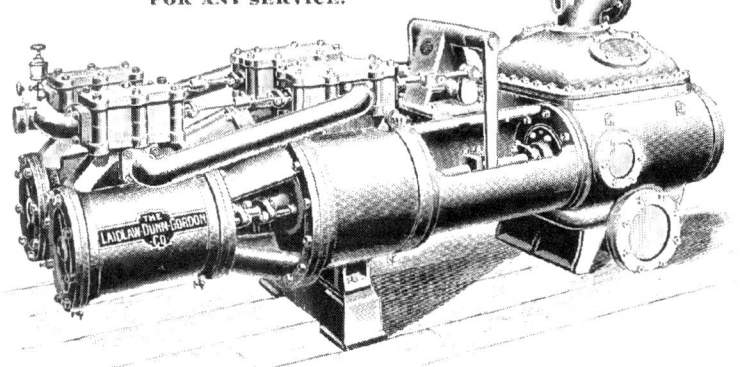

Water Works Pumping Engines, High Pressure, Compound, and Compound Condensing a Specialty.

The above Cut shows Pumping Engine at Norwood Water Works.

THOS. FORD   P. BARDO.

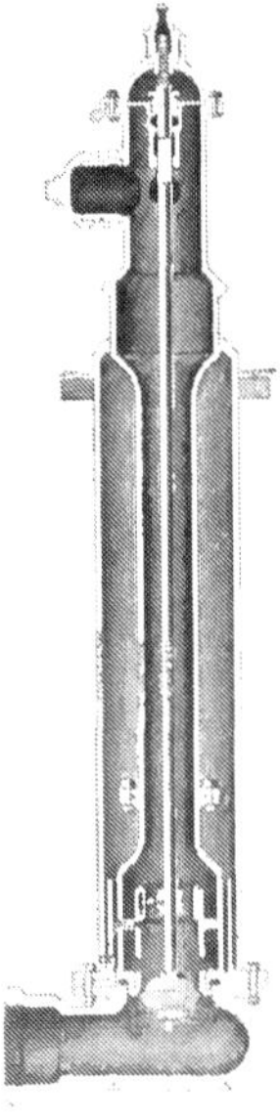

Bourbon Copper & Brass Works,

MANUFACTURERS OF

Fire Hydrants, Stop Valves

AND EXTENSION VALVE BOXES,

Copper and Brass Goods

OF EVERY DESCRIPTION.

IRON PIPE, CAST AND MALLEABLE IRON FITTINGS.

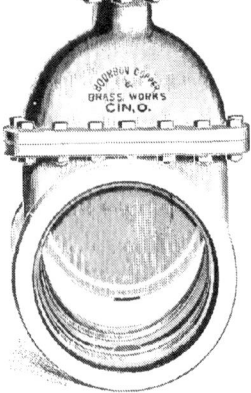

202 and 204 East Front Street,   - - -   CINCINNATI.

☞ CORRESPONDENCE SOLICITED.

Ohio's Largest Brewery

IS OWNED AND OPERATED BY

The Christian Moerlein Brewing Company

Brewers and Bottlers of The Finest Quality of **LAGER BEERS.**

CINCINNATI, OHIO.

The Moerlein Beers

ARE brewed from the choicest and most select MALT AND HOPS, are guaranteed to be GENUINE OLD LAGERS, and for PURITY, BRILLIANCY, TASTE and AROMA can not be excelled.

They are pronounced, without exaggeration, the most wholesome and invigorating beverages in the market, the favorable reception that has attended them wherever introduced being the most flattering evidence of their superiority.

Highest Awards at Chicago World's Fair, and all Cincinnati Expositions.

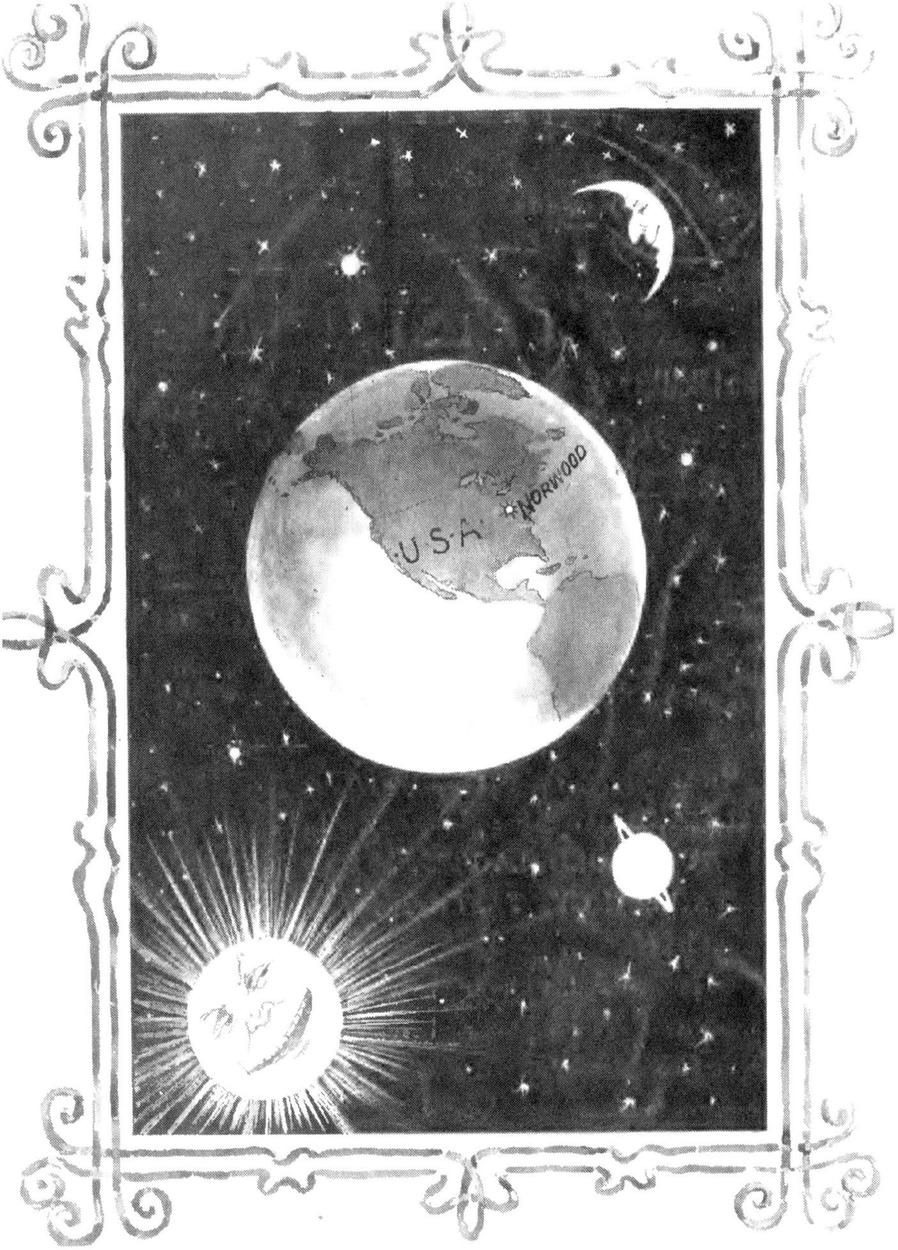
U.S.A.
NORWOOD